THE FARMINGTON COMMUNITY LIBRARY
FARMINGTON HILLS BRANCH
32737 West Twelve Mile Road

W9-DET-116

FREEDOM
RIDES

FREEDOM RIDES

JOURNEY FOR JUSTICE

JAMES HASKINS

30036000939916

HYPERION BOOKS FOR CHILDREN
NEW YORK

For Rosa Parks

ACKNOWLEDGMENTS

I am grateful to Kathy Benson, Deidre Grafel, and Ann Kalkhoff for their help. Special thanks to the Bayard Rustin Fund, Inc., and Walter Naegle, its executive director.

PHOTO CREDITS

Front jacket, pp. 35, 50, 58, 67, 81, 89, courtesy of UPI/Bettmann Photo Archives; pp. 5, 31, courtesy of the Schomberg Center for Research in Black Culture; p. 12 courtesy of the Bayard Rustin Fund, Inc.; p. 25 courtesy of Carl Iwasaki, Time-Life Picture Agency, © Time Inc; p. 70 courtesy of Wide World Photos.

Text © 1995 by James Haskins. All rights reserved. No part of this book may be used or reproduced in any manner whatsoever without written permission from the publisher. Printed in the United States of America. For information address Hyperion Books for Children, 114 Fifth Avenue, New York, New York 10011.

FIRST EDITION

1 3 5 7 9 10 8 6 4 2

Library of Congress Cataloging-in-Publication Data

Haskins, James
Freedom Rides/James Haskins—1st ed.
p. cm.
Includes bibliographical references and index.
ISBN 0-7868-0048-8—ISBN 0-7868-2037-3 (lib. bdg.)
1. Afro-Americans—Civil rights—Juvenile literature. 2. Civil
rights movements—Southern States—History—20th century—Juvenile
literature. 3. Southern States—Race relations—Juvenile
literature. [1. Afro-Americans—Civil rights. 2. Civil rights
movements—History. 3. Race relations.] I. Title.
E185.61.H335   1995
323.1′196073′075—dc20   94–7996

CONTENTS

THE FREEDOM TO RIDE

I was born and raised in Alabama at a time when the races were segregated, which really meant that black people were separated from and denied equal opportunities and accommodations with whites. I attended an all-black school. Our textbooks, gym equipment, and band instruments were castoffs from the white schools. We did not have an indoor gym and played our sports outdoors when weather permitted. Our band uniforms were paid for through bake sales and car washes, not provided by the county board of education as were the band uniforms for white students.

My family and I could not try on shoes in the white-owned stores downtown. We had to select what we wanted and hope they fit. We were served in the back of the store.

We could not go to white-owned restaurants. The public water fountains carried signs marked Whites Only and Colored. The public park was off-limits to blacks. Although I loved to read, I could not go to the public library. My mother had to ask a white woman friend to check out books from the library for me.

I did not think segregation was fair. It was painful and injurious and frustrating, and I resolved that if I ever had a chance to do something about those injustices, I would. In the meantime, I attended high school in Boston, Massachusetts, and escaped for a time the rigid segregation that had so infuriated me in Alabama. From afar, I applauded the efforts of Mrs. Rosa Parks and the black people of Montgomery, Alabama, who in 1955 boycotted that city's buses in protest over segregation and won a United States Supreme Court decision against bus segregation.

A few years after that victory, I enrolled at all-black Alabama State University in Montgomery, and while there I joined CORE (Congress of Racial Equality), at that time a small organization with only a few chapters.

One of the first actions CORE took after I joined was to test Interstate Commerce Commission laws that were intended to abolish racial discrimination against interstate passengers who patronized restaurants in the South. In the late 1950s, groups of riders, both white and black, went south on interstate buses and attempted to eat in restaurants with local blacks and whites. One of their stops was Montgomery, Alabama. Members of the Montgomery chapter of CORE were asked to join with the interstate riders at an integrated luncheon at the Regal Cafe, not far from the Alabama State University campus. As soon as we did, we were arrested and put in jail for violating the laws of the state of Alabama against whites and blacks eating together in public places.

The governor of Alabama, John Patterson, was the chief officer of the Alabama State University system, but it was the black president of the university who feared that the actions of his black students would have serious consequences for Alabama State. He expelled all eighteen of us, including Bernard Lee, who had served as an assistant to the Reverend Martin Luther King, Jr. The president gave as his reason that we were "out-of-state rabble-rousers," even though all of us were originally from Alabama. (Most of us had gone to northern or eastern high schools and returned only to go to Alabama State.)

After being expelled, most of us received scholarships to northern and Middle Atlantic universities. I was given a scholarship to Georgetown University in Washington, D.C., and it was then that I had to reenter the strange world of the Mason-Dixon line and of segregated interstate travel, of which I'd had a taste while I was attending school in Boston but returning to Alabama for visits.

Charles Mason and Jeremiah Dixon were English astronomers who established the borders of Maryland and Pennsylvania in 1767. Before the Civil War, the Mason-Dixon line that they established was used to distinguish free states from slave states. Since the Civil War it has been used to separate the North from the South on the eastern seaboard. In the days of racial segregation, it was just about at the Mason-Dixon line that black passengers traveling from the North along the eastern seaboard had to move to segregated bus seats or railroad cars.

When I was a college student traveling between Boston and Washington, D.C., I used to be amazed at how white the coach car became as the train approached the Mason-Dixon line. Many black passengers moved to the "colored" seating before they were required by law to do so, just to escape the indignity of being forced to move. African Americans traveling on the train from Boston, Philadelphia, or New York City could sit anywhere they wanted until they reached the Mason-Dixon line, but at Baltimore or thereabouts, all us black people were supposed to move to the "colored" section. The conductor would come through the train and say, "We are now crossing the Mason-Dixon line. All Negroes move to the rear!" In those days, all the conductors were white, usually Irish, and the Pullman porters were black. It seemed to me that while the conductors were nice until then, their attitude changed toward us, especially if some of us would not move. Sometimes it seemed as if they even enjoyed, indeed waited for, that moment when they could say those words, make us do something that they couldn't make us do—not by law, or force, or anything else—until then.

The African Americans who got on at Philadelphia going to Washington and points south seemed automatically to gravitate to the "correct" section of the train, almost as if they were born doing this, by rote, not thinking. But just about all the blacks made the move to the rear at some point, the poor blacks with their trunks and cardboard boxes tied with clothesline rope or hemp and their baskets of food, the well-dressed blacks with expensive luggage, proving they had done well up North, the students going on to Tuskegee, Morehouse, Spelman, and all the other Negro colleges along the line.

By the 1950s and 1960s, travel by air was an option, and there were no similar border changes of seating on airplanes. Of course, if African Americans had the money to fly, no one expected them to move.

Although there were many other types of segregation forced on African Americans, segregated transportation was in some ways the hardest type to endure, because it was so public. To maintain one's dignity, one could refuse to drink from the "colored" water fountains or use the "colored" public rest-room facilities, if those facilities were even available. But African Americans had to go to work (usually for whites) or visit relatives in another state or town, and so there was no way to avoid segregated transportation.

On segregated trains and buses, African Americans came up against a majority white culture that looked down on them and "kept them in their place" with segregation laws. In the nineteenth century, white trolley riders watched as African Americans stood on the street waiting for a "colored" car. In the twentieth century, white bus riders watched as African Americans were forced to pay their fare at the front door, then go around to the back door to board. White bus riders sat by as African American parents tried to explain to their children that they could not watch the driver because they were not allowed to sit up front. White bus riders who boarded after all the "white" seats in the front were filled demanded the seats of African Americans who were sitting down. It is no wonder that the fight against segregated transportation helped transform the civil rights protests of the 1950s and early 1960s into a civil rights *movement*. There was no more basic right than to be able to "ride free."

—Jim Haskins
    New York, 1995

CHAPTER ONE

THE EARLY FIGHT TO "RIDE FREE"

Back in the 1850s, New York City had laws providing for separate streetcars for blacks and whites. One Sunday afternoon in 1854, a black New York City schoolteacher named Elizabeth Jennings and her friend Sarah set off for church. At the corner of Chatham and Pearl streets in lower Manhattan, they boarded a horse-drawn Third Avenue Railway Company car. It was supposed to be for whites, for it did not have a sign that said Colored People Allowed in This Car. The conductor told them to leave and wait for "the car that had their people in it," which was about a block away. Elizabeth Jennings argued that they were late for church and that, besides, they were upstanding citizens. The conductor ordered the driver to stop and then hailed a policeman to help him get the women off. Rather than be roughed up, Jennings and her friend got off the car.

Jennings sued the Third Avenue Railway Company. A young white attorney named Chester A. Arthur represented her. It was his first case since earning his law degree and joining the law firm of Culver, Parker, and Arthur. (Arthur would later be elected president of the United States.) The case came to trial in 1855. Some members of the all-white jury argued that a black woman should not get the $500 in damages Jennings sought and agreed to award her only about half that amount. But they did decide that segregation on public transportation in the city of New York was wrong. For many years afterward, the black community of New York City celebrated February 22, the anniversary of the jury's decision, as a holiday.

At the time Elizabeth Jennings won her case, slavery was still legal in the southern United States. The Civil War (1861–65) was fought in part over the issue of slavery. After the northern states were victorious over the southern states that had tried to secede and set up a separate nation, slavery became illegal everywhere in the United States. An amendment to the United States Constitution, the Thirteenth, outlawing slavery, became law in 1865.

For some years afterward, northern troops occupied the vanquished rebel states until they wrote new state constitutions that guaranteed equal rights to African Americans. During this time of occupation, which was called Reconstruction, two other amendments to the Constitution were added. The Fourteenth Amendment (1868) declared all persons born or naturalized in the United States to be U.S. citizens and forbade any state to deprive any person of life, liberty, or property or deny them the equal protection of the laws. The Fifteenth Amendment (1870) guaranteed that the right of all U.S. citizens to vote would not be denied on account of "race, color, or previous condition of servitude."

The purpose of these amendments was to give African Americans the rights of full citizenship. The amendments were aimed especially at the southern states, where many former rebels would have preferred the return of slavery. During the Reconstruction period, blacks in the South were able to vote and hold office and enjoy many civil rights. But after about ten years, the federal troops pulled out, and slowly southern states began to take away most of the rights that had been given to blacks. Rather than denying blacks access to public transportation, for example, they instituted segregated cars and buses. Segregation laws came to be called Jim Crow laws after a comical minstrel character played by a white man in black makeup who called himself Jim Crow. Segregated railroad cars were called Jim Crow cars.

Before and during the Civil War, the idea of states' rights had become more popular throughout the nation. During the Reconstruction period, the federal government had overridden the idea of states' rights in favor of federal power. Now the pendulum of national opinion was swinging back the other way. A conflict over segregation on public transportation that went to the courts at the close of the nineteenth century set the legal precedent favoring states' rights in areas such as public transportation and segregation.

The case concerned public transportation in Louisiana. In 1890, the state legislature passed a law that required all railroad companies to provide "equal but separate accommodations for the white, and colored, races." The black community of New Orleans decided to challenge that law. As a test case, Homer Plessy, a light-skinned man who was described as "seven-eighths" white, boarded the white car of a train. When he was arrested for disobeying the segregation laws, he challenged the Louisiana law, saying that his civil rights were violated. After his arguments were rejected by the state courts, Plessy took his case to the U.S. Supreme Court, the highest court in the land. There, Plessy's attorneys argued on his behalf that the segregation law violated the requirement of the Fourteenth Amendment to the Constitution that "no state shall deny . . . the equal protection of the laws." The state of Louisiana argued, in turn, that "separate" was still "equal." In 1896 the Supreme Court ruled that "separate but equal" railroad cars were constitutional.

The Supreme Court decision in *Plessy v. Ferguson* did not

have a major effect in the northern states, where most segregation laws had been repealed before the Civil War. But it was a landmark in the southern fight against equal rights for black Americans. It was a signal for the white populations of the former Confederate states and other southern states to undo as much as possible the damage to their sense of privilege that had been caused by the defeat of the South in the Civil War and the outlawing of slavery. They could not bring slavery back, but they could make sure that blacks would be second-class citizens.

Because the Supreme Court decision in *Plessy v. Ferguson* concerned segregation on public transportation, transportation was the first area where it was strongly felt in the South. Before 1900, only Louisiana and Georgia had required separate seating for blacks and whites on streetcars. By 1905, North Carolina, Virginia, Alabama, Arkansas, South Carolina, Tennessee, Mississippi, Maryland, and Florida had enacted similar laws. Segregation also became the rule in railroad waiting rooms.

Southern blacks did not accept these segregation laws without a fight. In Montgomery, Alabama, in 1900, blacks boycotted the city's streetcars until the city council changed its ordinance so that nobody would be forced to give up a seat unless there was another seat available. But over the years, segregation set in anyway, although the ordinance against it remained on the books.

Gradually, the doctrine of "separate but equal" was applied in the South to most other areas of public life, from schools to drinking fountains, from public parks to public libraries. Some southern localities went so far as to bar blacks and whites from playing checkers together in public or from looking out the same factory windows.

African Americans hated all these laws, but those regulating

NEGRO EXPULSION FROM RAILWAY CAR. PHILADELPHIA.

Circa 1850, Philadelphia, Pennsylvania. A white conductor evicts a black passenger from an all-white railway car.

public transportation were especially hard on them. The railroad cars reserved for blacks were always in worse condition than those for whites. In cases where blacks and whites rode in the same cars, the section for blacks was always smaller than that for whites. Plus, laws were passed that made an entire railroad car a "white" car if necessary: When the white section filled up, blacks were required to give up their seats to standing white passengers. When bus transportation began to supplant train and trolley transportation, the same rules applied.

THE 1947 JOURNEY OF RECONCILIATION

By 1946, fifty years after the Supreme Court's decision in *Plessy v. Ferguson,* both the Court and the people of the United States had changed. The country had just emerged victorious from World War II, and there was a general sense of well-being and prosperity that brought a new generosity of spirit to many Americans.

African Americans had enlisted in large numbers in the armed services during World War II. They had fought well and bravely for freedom in Europe and the Pacific. When they returned to the same old segregation at home, not just they, but some whites, believed that it was unfair and that something should be done about the segregation laws.

Those white Americans included Harry S. Truman, president of the United States. In December 1946, President Truman set up a President's Commission on Civil Rights "to determine whether and in what respect . . . the authority and means possessed by the federal, state and local governments may be strengthened and improved to safeguard the rights of the people."

The following June, Truman spoke at the annual convention of the National Association for the Advancement of Colored People (NAACP), the first president to do so. He stated, "We must make the federal government a friendly, vigilant defender of the rights and equalities of all Americans. And again, I mean *all* Americans."

The branch of the federal government that seemed most willing to guarantee equal rights was the United States Supreme Court, the same body that had ruled in favor of segregation in the *Plessy* case half a century before. The nine men who now sat on the Court had different attitudes. None of the nine was prepared to attack the laws of individual states. But the Court could do something about practices that involved more than one state, such as interstate travel.

Southern segregation laws caused some strange practices in cases of travel from one state to another. On interstate buses, for example, black passengers boarding in Pennsylvania could sit anywhere. But once they crossed the border into a segregated region, such as Washington, D.C., they would have to move to the back of the bus. The same was true on trains. At Washington, D.C., all blacks traveling from the North had to get off and board another train or another coach on the same train.

In Virginia, a black woman named Irene Morgan challenged this practice on interstate buses. She was arrested for not moving to the back of an interstate bus once it entered the South, even though she was holding an interstate bus ticket. On June 3, 1946, the U.S. Supreme Court ruled in *Morgan v. Commonwealth of Virginia* that segregation on interstate buses was unconstitutional. In its opinion, the Court stated that segregation of passengers crossing state lines was an "undue burden on interstate commerce."

In a later decision by the Court of Appeals for the District of Columbia, the *Morgan* decision was applied to interstate train travel as well as bus travel. A civil rights organization called the Congress of Racial Equality (CORE) decided to see if the Supreme Court decision was being obeyed in the South.

CORE had been founded in 1942 with the assistance of an older organization called the Fellowship of Reconciliation (FOR). Because the FOR was concerned with pacifist (nonviolent and anti-war) causes, it could not be true to its intent and philosophy and yet engage in confrontational actions.

James Farmer, the young race-relations secretary of the FOR who had recently graduated from Howard University with a degree in theology, was the one who first approached the FOR with the idea of founding an organization that would fight racial discrimination using the same techniques that Mohandas K. Gandhi was using in India.

Nonviolent protest to bring about social change was achieving positive results in India, where Indians of all castes, or classes, had united to secure their independence from Great Britain. Beginning in 1915 and led by Mohandas K. Gandhi, who was called the Mahatma, or Great Soul, by his followers, Indians resisted British laws and did not try to defend themselves when they were beaten, arrested, or jailed. The jails of India were filled to overflowing, but this only served to attract more Indians to the cause. It took many long years, but Gandhi's "soul force" eventually won out, causing Britain at last to surrender India to the Indians in 1947.

Although the FOR had decided against sponsoring the project directly, Farmer was authorized to establish the new organization while he continued to work for the FOR. In 1942, with several others, including FOR staff member Bayard Rustin, Farmer helped found the Congress of Racial Equality among black and white students at the University of Chicago.

CORE's purpose was to fight racial injustice wherever it was found, and CORE was to take a more confrontational tack than older civil rights organizations, such as the NAACP and the

National Urban League. Years later, Farmer recalled that an official of the Chicago Urban League described the differences among the organizations this way: "the Urban League is the State Department of civil rights; the NAACP is the War Department; and CORE is the marines."[1]

CORE's first project was to desegregate a roller-skating rink called White City on the South Side of Chicago. While that ultimately successful campaign was in progress, word of the new organization quickly spread, and chapters sprang up in other cities. To celebrate its first national conference, in June 1943, CORE staged a sit-in at Stoners, an expensive all-white restaurant in Chicago. Sixty-five people entered the restaurant and sat down, and refused to leave until they were served. The management of the restaurant gave in and agreed to change its segregation policies. The members of the young organization, elated by their victory, vowed to continue to fight injustice with such protests.

For the next few years they did so, mostly on a small scale and on the local level. But after the Supreme Court decision in *Morgan v. Commonwealth of Virginia,* leaders of CORE and the Racial-Industrial Committee of the FOR decided to launch a protest whose effects would be felt nationally. They voted to jointly sponsor a Journey of Reconciliation through the upper South to see if bus and train companies were following the *Morgan* decision.

While the Journey of Reconciliation was very courageous for its time, it was not reckless. For one thing, those who undertook the journey did not go into the Deep South, where racism was worst. Instead, they confined their journey to the states of the upper South, where contact with northern states contributed to more liberal racial viewpoints. For another, only men went on the journey. Women like Irene Morgan might stand up for their own rights and later be plaintiffs in suits against segregation on public transit, but when it came to confronting segregation laws and practices, women were not considered for frontline positions by the almost exclusively male leadership of civil rights and pacifist organizations.

Sixteen men participated in the Journey of Reconciliation, either full- or part-time. They were both black and white. The black participants included Bayard Rustin, who was in his early thirties and had been working for the FOR for five years by the time he helped found CORE. Known for his strong organizational skills, he planned to keep a diary of the journey and was particularly interested, as he wrote later, to "learn the reaction of bus drivers, passengers, and police to those who nonviolently and persistently challenge Jim Crow in interstate travel."[2]

Other blacks among the group were Wallace Nelson, a freelance lecturer; Conrad Lynn, a New York attorney; Andrew Johnson, a student from Cincinnati, Ohio; Dennis Banks, a Chicago musician; William Worthy, who worked for the New York Council for the Permanent Fair Employment Practices Commission; Eugene Stanley, a member of the faculty of the all-black North Carolina Agricultural and Technical College in Greensboro; and Nathan Wright, a church social worker from Cincinnati.

The white participants included George Houser, a staff member of the FOR and executive secretary of CORE; Ernest Bromley and Louis Adams, Methodist ministers from North Carolina; James Peck, editor of the Workers Defense League *News Bulletin;* Igal Roodenko, a New York horticulturalist; Worth Randle, a Cincinnati botanist; Joseph Felmet, a member of the Southern Workers Defense League; and Homer Jack, executive secretary of the Chicago Council Against Racial and Religious Discrimination.

Because the whites in the group were not directly affected by segregation, they had to have a higher motive for putting themselves in the path of danger. Several of them were Jews who believed strongly in the need to fight against discrimination wherever it occurred in order that horrors such as the recent Holocaust in Europe would never happen again. Members of organizations such as the Southern Workers Defense League and the Chicago Council Against Racial and Religious Discrimination had already committed themselves to working for human equality. James Peck was somewhat unique, however. An heir to the Peck and Peck clothier fortune, he was an idealist who had shocked his Harvard freshman class in 1933 by arriving at a dance with a Negro date. He had since chosen to devote his life to helping those less fortunate than he.

Ministers, too, might be expected to have a strong urge to work for their fellow human beings, but in the 1940s the Methodist church was the only church that had a strong commitment to activism in this area. But a horticulturalist? Perhaps one reason why Igal Roodenko was involved was that he had a deep appreciation of life itself, and thus of the quality of life of all human beings.

Roodenko was a very good friend of Bayard Rustin's, who years later described him as a well-meaning fellow, who had served time in jail as a conscientious objector (against all war), but very timid. According to Rustin, he spent six months convincing Roodenko to join the Journey of Reconciliation before his friend finally agreed.

Because some of the men could only participate part-time, all sixteen were never on the same bus. But at all times between eight and ten men did participate. This level of involvement made it possible for the Journey of Reconciliation to be made in two parts, either to make two separate tests on the same bus line or to make tests on both Greyhound and Trailways buses. Greyhound and Trailways were chosen because they were the two major interstate bus lines.

1947, Richmond, Virginia. Some of the Freedom Riders who participated in the Journey of Reconciliation. From left to right: Worth Randle, Wallace Nelson, Ernest Bromley, James Peck, Igal Roodenko, Bayard Rustin, Joseph Felmet, George Houser, and Andrew Johnson.

The following account is based on the notes of Bayard Rustin, who kept a diary of the Journey of Reconciliation and later made a full report with George Houser:

On April 9, 1947, two groups, including both whites and blacks, boarded Trailways and Greyhound buses in Washington, D.C., bound for Richmond, Virginia. On both trips, the blacks sat in front and the whites in back. The bus drivers said nothing, and the other passengers paid little attention. In fact, a white couple sat on the backseat of the Greyhound with two blacks, and a black woman took a seat beside a young white man in the center of the bus when she could have taken a vacant seat next to a black man.

On April 10, two groups, again including both whites and blacks, boarded a Trailways and a Greyhound bus for a trip from Richmond to Petersburg, Virginia. On the Greyhound, the other passengers stared at the black men riding up front but did not say anything. On the Trailways, a black passenger spoke to two black Journeyers, saying that a Negro might be able to get away with riding up front in that part of the country but that some bus drivers were crazy and that "the farther South you go, the crazier they get." Two black women noticed white James Peck sitting in the rear of the bus reading his *New York Times* and laughed, "He wouldn't know what it was all about if he was asked to move."

The following day, April 11, Conrad Lynn, the black New York attorney, was arrested on the Trailways bus bound for Raleigh, North Carolina, before it left the Petersburg station. Although Lynn explained that the *Morgan* decision allowed him to sit at the front of the bus, the bus driver was insistent that he had to follow the company rules on segregation and called the police.

The local magistrate did not want to bother with the case. When finally issued, the warrant against Lynn was for disorderly conduct. He was released on $25 bond. During the more than two-hour wait, the other passengers were patient for the most part. A black porter at the bus station made the only complaint, saying of Lynn, "What's the matter with him? He's crazy. Where does he think he is? We know how to deal with him. We ought to drag him off."

Later on the same day, James Peck and Bayard Rustin boarded a Greyhound bus bound for Durham, North Carolina, and sat together up front. About ten miles out of Petersburg, the driver told Rustin to move. When Rustin refused, the bus driver said he would attend to the matter at Blackstone, Virginia. But after the driver talked with other bus drivers at Blackstone, he made no move against Rustin and continued on to Clarksville, Virginia. There, the group changed buses. Nothing happened until the bus reached Oxford, North Carolina. There, the bus driver summoned the police, but they refused to arrest Rustin. Other passengers waiting to get on at Oxford were not allowed to do so. Only a black schoolteacher from Oxford was permitted to board, because he had offered to plead with Rustin to move. The middle-aged teacher said to Rustin, "Please move. Don't do this. You'll reach your destination either in front or in back. What difference does it make?" Rustin explained his reason for not moving and was supported by other black passengers on the bus.

When it became clear that Rustin was not going to move, the bus continued on to Durham. There, the black schoolteacher pleaded with James Peck not to use his name in any reports about the incident. "It will hurt me in the community," he said. "I'll never do it again."

On the Trailways bus from Raleigh, North Carolina, to Chapel Hill, North Carolina, on April 12, Conrad Lynn and Wallace Nelson, both black, rode together on the double seat in front of the very rear seat. It was a crowded bus, and when two white college men got on, the driver asked the two to move to the rear seat so the two white men could sit down. When they refused, saying they were interstate passengers, he said the matter would be handled in Durham. A white passenger asked the driver if he needed help, but the driver said, "No, we don't want to handle it this way." By the time the bus reached Durham, many white passengers had gotten off, and the driver did not press the issue.

Meanwhile, also on April 12, the Rustin-Peck group boarded a Trailways bus from Durham to Chapel Hill. Andrew Johnson, the black student from Cincinnati, and Rustin sat in the second seat from the front. Almost immediately, the driver asked them to move to the rear of the bus. When they did not, the driver called the stationmaster to repeat the order. Five minutes later, policemen arrived to arrest Johnson and Rustin on charges of refusing to move when ordered to do so. James Peck, who was seated in the middle of the bus, got up and said to the police, "If you arrest them you'll have to arrest me, too, for I'm going to sit in the rear." The stationmaster told the police to arrest Peck, too.

The three men were taken to the police station and held for thirty minutes, then released without charge when an attorney arrived to represent them. A Trailways official also arrived and told the police that the company knew an interracial group was making a test of the interstate bus laws. He told the police, "We know all about this. Greyhound is letting them ride. But we're not." CORE and the FOR determined to sue Trailways and the police of Durham for false arrest. But they also canceled one of two planned tests on Trailways buses from Chapel Hill to Greensboro, North Carolina, on April 13 because of events on the Trailways bus the previous day.

Andrew Johnson and Joseph Felmet, the white worker with the Southern Workers Defense League, boarded a Trailways bus in

Chapel Hill bound for Greensboro on April 13 and sat in the second seat from the front. The driver asked them to move as soon as Felmet boarded. The police station was just across the street from the bus station, and so the police arrived to arrest them in no time. Johnson went with the police immediately. Felmet did not get up to accompany the police right away, because he wanted to make sure there were witnesses to the arrest, so CORE could later file a suit for false arrest. The police pulled him up and shoved him out of the bus.

All the bus drivers carried witness cards, so in case there was an accident, passengers could report what they saw. The driver on this bus distributed witness cards so the passengers could report what they had seen in this case of nonviolent protest. One young white woman told the driver, "You don't want me to sign one of these. I'm a damn Yankee and I think this is an outrage."

Bayard Rustin and Igal Roodenko, the New York horticulturalist, took this as a sign that at least some of the other passengers were in sympathy with the Journey of Reconciliation protest. They moved to the seats that had been vacated by Johnson and Felmet, causing much discussion among the other passengers.

The driver had been off the bus at the time. When he returned, he ordered Rustin and Roodenko to move. They refused, and he had them arrested as well. A southern white woman seated at the front of the bus gave her name and address to Rustin as he walked by her.

All four men were booked by the police and released on $50 bonds. They then returned to the bus station, having been delayed almost two hours. White taxi drivers waiting at the bus station were becoming angered by the events. One of them approached James Peck and hit him, accusing him of "coming down here to stir up the niggers."

When the four men who had been arrested left the police station, they were picked up by a local white Presbyterian minister, the Reverend Charles Jones, who drove them to his home. Two cabs filled with taxi men followed, and in front of Jones's home they threw rocks and waved sticks at the interracial group. But they did not attack the house.

Moments after the group entered the minister's house, the telephone rang and an anonymous voice told Jones, "Get those damn niggers out of town or we'll burn your house down. We'll be around to see that they go." Although Jones called the police, who came in about twenty minutes, the Journeyers decided it was best to leave town before nightfall. Two cars took them to Durham by way of Greensboro so they could attend a scheduled meeting in Durham.

On April 14, two tests were made on Greyhound buses bound for Winston-Salem, North Carolina. No incidents occurred, suggesting that the Greyhound policy of noninterference was being upheld. There were also no incidents the following day on a Greyhound bus from Winston-Salem to Asheville, North Carolina. But at Asheville, the group transferred to a Trailways bus, and Wallace Nelson, the black freelance lecturer, who was sitting close to the front, was told by the driver to move to the rear. Nelson explained that he was holding an interstate ticket and could sit wherever he wanted, by ruling of the U.S. Supreme Court. The driver did not make him move, but at almost every stop at every small town after that, the driver had to explain why Nelson was sitting where he was. Other passengers were not pleased, but did nothing.

On April 17, on a Trailways bus from Asheville, North Carolina, to Knoxville, Tennessee, black Chicago musician Dennis Banks and white editor of the Workers Defense League *News Bulletin* James Peck sat in the second seat. Banks was asked to move before the bus even left the station because a white passenger had complained about him to the bus driver. After Banks explained that he was an interstate passenger, the driver summoned the police. Banks was arrested. Peck objected that he was not also arrested, saying, "We're traveling together, and you will have to arrest me, too." When the police did not do so, he moved to the rear. They then arrested him.

The two men were booked at the city jail and released on $100 bond each, with a trial date set for the following day.

On April 18, Judge Sam Cathay heard the case in police court. Curtis Todd, a black attorney from Winston-Salem, represented Banks and Peck, for there were no black attorneys in Asheville; in fact, Todd was the first black attorney ever to appear in that court. Neither the judge nor the state's attorney knew about the Supreme Court's *Morgan* decision and had to borrow attorney Todd's copy to read. The judge didn't seem to care and asked what the maximum sentence was under North Carolina law for disorderly conduct and levied that maximum sentence, thirty days in jail each.

Meanwhile, Journeyers on a Greyhound bus from Asheville to Knoxville the same day encountered no difficulties. They traveled on Greyhound within Tennessee for the next two days, without incident.

On April 19, Cincinnati church social worker Nathan Wright and Homer Jack, white executive secretary of the Chicago Council Against Racial and Religious Discrimination, tested segregation on a white train coach from Nashville, Tennessee, to Louisville, Kentucky. The conductor ordered Wright to go to the Jim Crow car. He refused, and the conductor said, "If we were in Alabama, I and the other passengers would throw you out the window." He threatened to have Wright arrested, but no arrest was made. After the conductor left, a white woman sitting nearby gave her name and address and offered to help if needed.

Between April 19 and April 21, several tests were made on Greyhound buses and on the Norfolk and Western Railway, in Ohio, Virginia, and Washington, D.C. There were no important incidents. The Journey of Reconciliation was nearing its end.

Then, on April 22, several Journeyers boarded a Trailways bus in Lynchburg, Virginia, bound for Washington, D.C. Black free-lance lecturer Wallace Nelson and white FOR staff member George Houser sat down at the front of the bus. About five miles out of Lynchburg, the bus driver noticed Nelson, and when he stopped at a service station he asked Nelson to move to the rear. Nelson refused, saying he was an interstate passenger, and Houser explained that they were traveling together. The driver said they could ride in the rear in that case. But, asked Houser, wouldn't that also break the Jim Crow segregation rules? The driver said that Houser would have to sit one seat in front of Nelson in the rear. The two men refused, and the driver, apologizing profusely, had Nelson, but not Houser, arrested in the small town of Amherst, Virginia. When Houser got off the bus to post bond for Nelson, the driver was again very apologetic.

Nelson and Houser then took a train on the Southern Railway at Amherst. As they got on, they asked the conductor where they could ride together. He answered that it was against the rules for them to ride anywhere together. The two chose to sit together in the Jim Crow car. The driver threatened to have them arrested, but did not follow through on the threat.

On April 23, black Chicago musician Dennis Banks boarded a Trailways bus in Charlottesville, Virginia, and sat in the front. Whites James Peck and the Cincinnati botanist Worth Randle also boarded and sat on the rear seat. For two hours out of Charlottesville, the driver said nothing. Then, in Culpeper, Virginia, he told Banks to move to the rear. He made no move against the two white men in the back, even though they, too, were violating the bus company's segregation laws. Banks was arrested and then released on a $25 bond.

The Journey of Reconciliation ended as planned on April 23, 1947, and in the opinion of Bayard Rustin, the people of the upper South were prepared for change. "The situation in the upper South is in a great state of flux," he reported. In parts where blacks had demonstrated great resistance to Jim Crow laws, many racial barriers had already come down. "One has reason to believe," he wrote, "that when in the other areas there has been as much a concentrated education effort and non-violent resistance has occurred . . . conditions will equally improve."

The Journey of Reconciliation was very risky for its time. Never before had an integrated group traveled through the upper South to test compliance with antisegregation laws. There had been little violence and comparatively few arrests. But the unpleasantness that had occurred on the Trailways buses had caused the CORE and FOR leadership to curtail the Journey on that line.

Furthermore, because there was such fear on the part of local black officials, the Journeyers who had been arrested—and who had expected to mount a successful legal challenge based on the Supreme Court decision—received little help from these officials and ended up serving time on southern chain gangs.

Rustin and his friend Roodenko had been arrested in Chapel Hill, North Carolina, on April 12. Promised representation by lawyers for the NAACP, they expected to plead not guilty and avoid prison. But two days before they were to return to North Carolina for trial, Roy Wilkins, head of the NAACP, called Rustin with some bad news.

"You've got to go on the chain gang, because we are not going to make a case," Wilkins said. "We are going to ask you to plead guilty." When Rustin asked why, Wilkins explained that the local black attorney whom the NAACP expected to represent the Journeyers claimed he had lost the stubs of the tickets proving that they were interstate passengers. It was clear that the real story was that he had been paid off by local whites to lose the stubs.

Explaining how a black attorney could have betrayed the Journeyers, Rustin once said, "This was a period similar to that in South Africa today, where for every black who was a resistor there were two or three blacks in every community who, because of fear or poverty or miseducation or cowardice—or for money—were prepared to be spies."[3] Without proof, Rustin and Roodenko had no case.

Rustin recalled years later that in March 1948, when he and the three others who had been arrested in Chapel Hill—Andrew S. Johnson, Joseph A. Felmet, and Igal Roodenko—came before Judge Chester A. Morris in Hillsborough, North Carolina, the judge told Rustin, "Well, I know you're a poor, misled nigra from the North. Therefore, I'm going to give you thirty days on the chain gang." Then the judge turned angrily to the timid horticulturalist Igal Roodenko. "Mr. Rodenky," he said, purposely mispronouncing Roodenko's name, "I presume you're Jewish, Mr. Rodenky. It's about time you white Jews from New York learned that you can't come down here bringing your nigras with you to upset the customs of the South. Now, just to teach you a lesson, I gave your black boy thirty days on the chain gang, now I give you ninety."

Years later, Rustin would joke to his friend, "Well, you see, there are some advantages to being black," and Roodenko would laugh.[4]

The other white, Joseph Felmet, was also sentenced to a chain gang, while Johnson was merely fined $25. All three appealed their sentences, but after two years of litigation their arrests were upheld by higher courts. When the Supreme Court of North Carolina ruled against them, the three voluntarily returned to North Carolina to do their time.

Rustin used his time on the North Carolina chain gang (he was let off after only twenty-two days because of good behavior) to advantage. He took notes on his own experiences and those of fellow prisoners and had the notes smuggled out of the camp in Roxboro, North Carolina. After his return to New York, he wrote extensively about the inhuman conditions for prisoners on the gangs. His account was serialized in the *New York Post* and caused considerable debate about chain gangs. Within two years, chain gangs were abolished in North Carolina.

THE *BROWN V. BOARD OF EDUCATION* DECISION

Meanwhile, civil rights groups and their attorneys were fighting segregation in the South on another front, that of education. A free public education was one of the most basic rights that white Americans took for granted, but the same right was not available to black Americans.

Since the time of slavery, when teaching slaves to read and write was illegal in some states, black people had believed that if they could get a good education, they would be able to break down at least some of the barriers placed in front of them. But while a free public education had been guaranteed to southern blacks since the Civil War and the abolition of slavery, that education had never been of the same quality as that available to whites.

Black schools were nearly always housed in black churches or in ramshackle structures that were cold in the winter and hot in the summer. White schools were actual school buildings built and paid for by local governments and better equipped with supplies. While county governments paid for fuel for white schools, they did not do the same for black schools, forcing black parents to donate wood and haul it to the schools themselves.

White schools always had newer equipment and textbooks;

black schools had to make do with castoffs from the white schools. White schools had gyms and libraries; black schools rarely did. White students who lived far away from school were transported by school buses; black students had to walk to school, no matter how many miles away it was.

The black school year was shorter than the white school year. Most black schools were in session for only five months, to allow black children to work in the fields from early spring to late fall.

Most southern towns had white high schools, because white students were expected to continue their schooling after the elementary grades. The same was not expected of black students, and those who wished to attend high school had to go to the larger cities. If the state colleges for blacks did not offer the courses a black student needed, then he or she would have to go to college out of state, for no white college in the state would admit black students.

Since the 1930s, attorneys working for the NAACP had brought suits in the courts over segregated education, charging that the idea expressed in the *Plessy v. Ferguson* opinion, that separate facilities were legal as long as they were equal, was not being followed. They had sued for equal pay for black teachers. They had sued to get black students admitted to graduate schools, charging that if a state had no law school for blacks and would not admit blacks to its white law school, then that was a clear case of discrimination. Based on their successes in many of these suits, the NAACP's lawyers decided to take a greater risk: to attack the very notion of separate but equal.

Led by Thurgood Marshall, who had once himself been denied admission to the University of Maryland's law school because he was black, the NAACP attorneys decided that they need not continue trying to fight against segregation in *physical* facilities but should take steps to prove that separate facilities by their very nature could never be equal.

Marshall and other NAACP lawyers brought suit simultaneously in four states—South Carolina, Kansas, Virginia, and Delaware. When state court rulings went against them in all cases but Delaware, Marshall and the others appealed those decisions to the United States Supreme Court. The Court agreed to hear the case called *Brown v. Board of Education.*

1953, Topeka, Kansas. Linda Brown, the daughter of the principal plaintiff in the 1954 *Brown v. Board of Education* Supreme Court case, stands outside the Monroe School.

The case had first been brought in Topeka, Kansas, in the late 1940s by the Reverend Oliver Brown, whose seven-year-old daughter, Linda, had to cross railroad tracks to wait for a rattletrap bus to take her to a black school. Brown sued the local schoolboard to gain his daughter's admittance to the white school. By the time it reached the U.S. Supreme Court, the case had taken on much greater dimensions than the safety of one little girl.

Thurgood Marshall and his associates called expert witnesses to testify that being segregated caused black children to feel that they were inferior to white children, and that to insist on giving them a separate education was to strike a blow at them at a young age, a blow from which they would never recover. All of the justices agreed, voting 9–0 in their decision, which was handed down on May 17, 1954. The decision read in part: "We must consider public education in the light of its full development and its present place in American life throughout the nation. . . . Today it is a principal instrument in awakening the child to cultural values, in preparing him for later professional training, and in helping him to adjust normally. . . . We conclude that in the field of public education the doctrine of 'separate but equal' has no place."

It was a landmark decision, and one that would have wide application to other areas of American life. If segregation was wrong in education, then it was also wrong in where people lived, where they could sit on buses, where they could get jobs, where they could get medical care, and where they could swim and play baseball.

But the decision in *Brown v. Board of Education* was no magic wand that the Court waved over the nation, instantly turning all whites into fair-minded individuals. White southerners resisted integration at every turn.

In Prince Edward County, Virginia, for example, the county government transferred most of its school property to hastily organized private schools for white children. That left the black children with no white public schools to integrate. In other parts of the South, local authorities barred blacks from entering previously white schools, making it necessary for the federal government to call out the National Guard. As black demands for civil rights increased, so did white violence.

But for African Americans active in the cause of civil rights, there was no turning back. The *Brown* decision was a major blow to segregation, and more and more tests of segregation in every area of southern life were to come.

THE MONTGOMERY BUS BOYCOTT OF 1955

"I don't think any segregation law angered black people in Montgomery more than bus segregation," says Rosa Parks, speaking of the law the state of Alabama passed in 1945 that required all bus companies to enforce segregation. "Here it was, half a century after the first segregation law, and there were 50,000 African Americans in Montgomery. More of us rode the buses than Caucasians did, because more whites could afford cars. It was very humiliating having to suffer the indignity of riding segregated buses twice a day, five days a week, to go downtown to work for white people."[1]

What was even more humiliating were the ridiculous practices expected of black people who used the Montgomery city buses. They had to climb up the stairs at the front door to pay their fare, then go around to the door at the side of the bus to board. They had to take seats at the back of the bus, and if it filled up, and there were white people standing in the aisles, they had to give up their seats to the white people.

The 1945 law was passed in Alabama as a result of an increasing number of incidents in which black people protested the segregation practices. Many of these incidents involved black soldiers who had returned from fighting in World War II. But some of them also involved black women who had not been to war.

In the spring of 1955 a teenage girl named Claudette Colvin and an elderly woman sitting in the middle section of a bus refused to give their seats up to white people. When the driver went to get the police, the elderly woman left the bus, but the teenage girl remained. The policemen dragged her from the bus and arrested her.

In response, a group of Montgomery blacks took a petition to the bus company and to city officials asking for better treatment. It did not ask for an end to segregation, just for an understanding that blacks would not have to give up their seats to whites when a bus became full. The Montgomery branch of the NAACP considered taking the case to federal court. Representatives met with Claudette Colvin about her being the plaintiff in the case, meaning that she would be the individual who would sue the bus company and the city. But the NAACP members wanted a plaintiff whose character could not be attacked, and Claudette Colvin was not that plaintiff. She was unmarried and pregnant, and back in the 1950s that meant she lacked moral character.

That summer, another teenage girl was arrested for refusing to obey the segregation laws. But she paid her fine and didn't protest. She was not interested in being a plaintiff in any federal case.

Rosa Parks was secretary of the Montgomery branch of the NAACP. She'd had her own run-ins with city bus drivers. Once, back in 1943, she had been put off a bus. When it pulled up to her stop, she saw that black people were crowded into the back and even standing on the steps leading up from the back door. Meanwhile, there were empty seats at the front. Instead of pushing through the people standing on the steps, she boarded the bus at the front.

The driver ordered her to get off the bus and go around to

the back door to get on. She refused. "Get off my bus!" he roared. Mrs. Parks got off, and from then on she made a point of not boarding that particular driver's bus again.

Over the years, she had heard the complaints of many black people about their treatment on the buses. She had talked with Claudette Colvin and understood why the NAACP did not pursue her case. "I knew they needed a plaintiff who was beyond reproach," she says, "because I was in on the discussions about possible court cases. But that is not why I refused to give up my bus seat to a white man on Thursday, December 1, 1955. I did not intend to get arrested. If I had been paying attention, I wouldn't even have gotten on that bus."[2]

Only after she had paid her fare did she realize that the bus driver was the same one who had put her off a bus twelve years earlier. She saw a vacant seat in the middle of the bus and sat down. A few stops later, more people boarded the bus. The white seats filled up, and one white man was left standing. The driver demanded the seats in the middle section of the bus where Rosa Parks was sitting. Other blacks in her row stood up, but Rosa Parks remained seated.

"People always say that I didn't give up my seat because I was tired," she says, "but that isn't true. I was not tired physically, or no more tired than I usually was at the end of a working day [she was a seamstress at a downtown department store]. I was not old, although some people have an image of me as being old then. I was forty-two. No, the only tired I was, was tired of giving in."[3]

The driver called the police, who escorted Mrs. Parks from the bus, arrested her, and took her to the nearest police station. Bailed out a few hours later by friends, she was ordered to appear for trial the following Monday.

Her associates in the NAACP, and other activist blacks in

Montgomery, were overjoyed about the incident. Mrs. Parks was the plaintiff they had been looking for: an upstanding, hardworking woman who was beyond reproach. As a young girl in the crowd cried out on the day Mrs. Parks appeared for trial, "Oh, she's so sweet. They've messed with the wrong one now."[4]

1955, Montgomery, Alabama. Rosa Parks (far right) participates at Highlander Folk School in a workshop on desegregation.

JoAnn Robinson was a teacher at the all-black Montgomery State College and a woman who had often protested segregation on the city's buses. When she heard of Mrs. Parks's arrest, she put out a handbill calling for the city's black citizens to boycott the buses the following Monday, when Mrs. Parks was scheduled to stand trial. Local NAACP leaders saw to it that the handbill was printed in the newspaper the *Montgomery Advertiser.* The ministers of local black churches devoted their sermons that Sunday to the indignities of bus segregation and urged their parishioners to observe the boycott.

The following Monday, December 5, 1955, the Montgomery city buses were practically empty, as black people walked to work, or took cabs, or carpooled. Local black leaders were overjoyed, because this was the first time ever that black citizens had joined together in massive protest of a segregation law. They vowed to continue the boycott until segregation on the city buses was ended.

Meanwhile, Mrs. Parks was found guilty, given a suspended sentence, and required to pay a small fine. The NAACP immediately filed an appeal, and over the next twelve months the case went to higher and still higher courts until finally it went all the way to the U.S. Supreme Court.

Just days into the boycott, local black leaders formed an organization called the Montgomery Improvement Association (MIA) to raise money to buy station wagons that the churches operated to take black people to work, to organize car pools, and to publicize the boycott. Bayard Rustin, who had helped organize and participated in the 1947 Journey of Reconciliation by the Congress of Racial Equality, traveled from New York to Montgomery to help with the organizing. The young minister of Dexter Avenue Baptist Church, Dr. Martin Luther King, Jr., was chosen as president of the MIA.

The main reason why King was chosen was that he was new to Montgomery and had not had time to make any strong friends or enemies. Unlike other ministers in town, he had not accepted favors from whites in Montgomery and so did not owe them anything. King soon showed that he was the best leader who could have been chosen, for he strongly believed in the principles of nonviolence.

While he was in college, King had read about Gandhi's campaign in India and had been inspired to hope that the same principles of nonviolence could be applied to the problem of segregation in his own country. Bayard Rustin was also a firm believer in nonviolence, and together they urged the blacks of Montgomery not to fight back, no matter what happened to them.

Whites in Montgomery tried everything to break the boycott. They fired their black employees who observed the boycott. They attacked and beat black cabdrivers. They bombed the homes of boycott leaders and made threatening telephone calls to others. King held frequent meetings at his church and other houses of worship to urge continued nonviolence. Remarkably, the blacks of Montgomery complied, even in the face of great personal risk.

The Montgomery bus boycott lasted just over a year, until December 20, 1956, when the actual written order came down from the Supreme Court that Montgomery's buses were no longer to be segregated. The following day, the black citizens of Montgomery returned to the buses.

By the time the boycott was over, Martin Luther King, Jr.'s name had become nationally known, and he went on to found a new civil rights organization, the Southern Christian Leadership Conference, and to become the most famous American civil rights leader of all time.

As for Mrs. Parks, she did not remain in Montgomery after the boycott. She and her husband, Raymond, received threatening telephone calls and feared for their safety, and so they moved to Detroit, Michigan. But her brave act inspired other southern blacks to demand their rights. In a few short years, the direct-action civil rights movement had begun in the South, with black people and their white supporters demonstrating against segregation and discrimination in all its forms. Many regarded Rosa Parks as the "mother of the movement."

THE CIVIL RIGHTS MOVEMENT BEGINS

As the new decade dawned, change was in the wind. The U.S. Supreme Court decision in *Brown v. Board of Education* and the success of the Montgomery bus boycott had inspired southern blacks to believe that real equality might at last be possible.

Following the Montgomery bus boycott, Martin Luther King, Jr., had organized a group of southern ministers to form the Southern Christian Leadership Conference (SCLC). Their first campaign was for voting rights for southern blacks, and on May 17, 1957, the third anniversary of the *Brown v. Board of Education* decision, they staged a Prayer Pilgrimage for Freedom in the nation's capital, Washington, D.C. There, in front of the Lincoln Memorial, King delivered his first public address to the entire nation, urging the president and Congress to "give us the ballot."

That August, President Dwight D. Eisenhower signed into law the first Civil Rights Act since the post–Civil War Reconstruction era. Although it aimed to guarantee basic rights to blacks, the law contained few provisions for doing so. Still, it was a start.

Meanwhile, blacks in many southern localities had brought suit against segregated schools, based on the 1954 Supreme Court decision, and in September 1957 President Eisenhower sent federal troops to Little Rock, Arkansas, to ensure that court-ordered integration of Central High School proceeded without interference.

But these occurrences were still sporadic, and black civil rights activists continued to work mostly through the courts and through moral persuasion.

Then, quite spontaneously, young people took up the cause. On February 1, 1958, students from the black North Carolina

1960, Greensboro, North Carolina. From left to right: Ronald Martin, Robert Patterson, and Mark Martin, students at North Carolina Agricultural and Technical College, participate in a sit-in at the Woolworth lunch counter.

Agricultural and Technical College in Greensboro staged a sit-in at a local segregated Woolworth's lunch counter and refused to leave until they were served. The sit-in movement spread like wildfire, and by February 10, black and white college students in ten southern cities were staging similar actions.

One of the strongest movements was started by students in Nashville, Tennessee, which had twelve colleges and universities. Diane Nash, a Chicagoan who attended all-black Fisk University; John Lewis, a native of Alabama who was a student at the American Baptist Theological Seminary; a fellow seminarian named James Bevel; and others formed an organization they called the Nashville Student Movement. Firm believers in the principles of nonviolence, they were taught by James Lawson, a thirty-two-year-old divinity student at Vanderbilt University who was active in the Fellowship of Reconciliation—the same organization that had promoted Gandhian techniques of passive resistance and helped found CORE back in the 1940s. The Nashville students drew up this list of rules for behavior at sit-ins:

> Don't strike back if cursed or abused.
> Don't laugh out.
> Don't hold conversations with your fellow workers.
> Don't leave your seats until your leader has given you
>   instructions to do so.
> Don't block entrances to the stores and the aisles.
> Show yourself courteous and friendly at all times.
> Sit straight and always face the counter.
> Report all serious incidents to your leader.
> Refer all information to your leader in a polite manner.
> Remember love and nonviolence.
> May God bless each of you.

They were dedicated to those principles and to maintaining their dignity at all costs.

"We would dress up in a coat and tie," Lewis has recalled. "We would sit there all day. Someone would spit on you. Someone would pour drinks on you. They would call the white demonstrators 'nigger lovers.' But no one would strike back."[1]

Lewis was motivated not only by a knowledge of the injustice of segregation but also by a firm religious belief. Born in rural Alabama, son of a sharecropper, Lewis was in charge of tending the family's chickens. His family could not afford the $18.95 incubator advertised in the Sears, Roebuck catalog, so he marked the eggs with a pencil in order to tell which ones were ready to hatch a little early. He would then pull them out so the hen would stay on the nest with the others.

Lewis preached his first sermons to the chickens. He also presided over baptisms and funerals of chickens. During that period of his life, he refused to eat chicken at his family's dinner table.

Lewis wanted to attend Troy State College in Alabama, but the school did not admit blacks. That's how he ended up at American Baptist Theological Seminary in Nashville and how he became, at the age of twenty-one, a civil rights protester.

Seeing the potential power of this grassroots student action, Ella Baker and others active in the SCLC, as well as Diane Nash and others in the Nashville Student Movement, helped the students organize the Student Nonviolent Coordinating Committee (SNCC, pronounced "snick"), in Raleigh, North Carolina. Other veteran civil rights organizations realized that if they did not also begin to take direct action against segregation, the young civil rights workers were going to leave them behind.

THE FREEDOM RIDES BEGIN

Of the established civil rights organizations, the Congress of Racial Equality (CORE) was in the best position to act quickly, for although it was the tiniest and least well funded, it already had a tradition of direct action dating back to its desegregation campaigns of the early 1940s and the Journey of Reconciliation in 1947. Moreover, it had a brand-new national director named James Farmer, whose long association with CORE made him eager to see it publicly known in a big way. CORE had been Farmer's idea originally, and he had helped establish the organization in Chicago in 1942.

In the intervening years, Farmer had worked as an organizer for the American Federation of Labor's Upholsterers' International Union, as student secretary of the League for Industrial Democracy, and at District Council 37 in New York City. In 1959, he had joined the national staff of the NAACP. But all the while, he, his wife, and a few close friends, including James Peck, had kept CORE quietly alive. Then, in 1961, it seemed to all who still believed in CORE that it was time for the organization to play a major role in the emerging civil rights movement. Farmer was persuaded to leave his job at the NAACP and devote his full attention to CORE.

At the first CORE staff meeting over which Farmer presided

as national director, staff member Gordon Carey suggested that CORE undertake a second Journey of Reconciliation to test compliance with a new Supreme Court decision. That decision, handed down in December 1960 in the case of *Boynton v. Virginia,* held that segregation in waiting rooms and restaurants serving interstate bus passengers was unconstitutional. Carey's idea was to send an interracial group of people trained in nonviolence on a bus ride through the entire South, testing bus facilities. There was no question that they would encounter violent resistance, and the resulting publicity would give CORE a national platform. Farmer agreed that it was a good idea. He believed that the federal government did not intend to enforce the law because officials in the administration of the new president, John F. Kennedy, feared losing the support of southern Democrats. In fact, he believed that the only way to get the federal government to enforce the law was to, as he put it, "make it more dangerous politically for the federal government not to enforce federal law than for them to enforce federal law."[1]

Farmer decided not to have a second Journey of Reconciliation but rather a Freedom Ride, which soon expanded to Freedom Ride*s*.

Thirteen people volunteered to be Freedom Riders, men and women, black and white, ranging in age from twenty-one to sixty. Several were CORE staff members, including Farmer and James Peck. Peck, who had been on the Journey of Reconciliation fourteen years before, had since then served as editor of one of CORE's publications. Two black members of SNCC had volunteered—John Lewis, the youngest of the group, and Henry Thomas, a student at Howard University in Washington, D.C.

The oldest volunteers were white—sixty-year-old Walter Bergman and his wife, Frances. Bergman was a professor at Wayne

State University in Detroit and a teachers union activist who had been in Socialist party politics in the 1920s and 1930s.

They underwent three days of training in nonviolence in Washington, D.C. Then, on May 4, 1961, they separated into two groups and boarded a Greyhound and a Trailways bus, sitting in various parts of each bus and in various combinations—some whites in back, some blacks in front, and at least one interracial pair sitting together.

Although CORE had notified the press, few in the media paid much attention to the announced Freedom Ride. Simeon Booker of *Jet* magazine had decided to accompany the riders and had personally told U.S. attorney general Robert F. Kennedy, who also happened to be the president's brother, that he expected trouble. But the Kennedys had not paid much attention either.

Whites in the communities through which the buses would travel did not know about the Freedom Rides. However, many blacks did; they had been notified through a network of ministers and civil rights activists. Some had already planned meetings, rallies, and overnight accommodations for the riders and stood ready to aid the riders in any way they could if there was trouble.

The Freedom Riders sang freedom songs as the buses started on their way. The first stop was Fredericksburg, Virginia, where White and Colored signs were posted in the bus station's waiting room and restaurant, although the Supreme Court's *Boynton* decision now outlawed them. But no one bothered the riders. Nothing happened in Richmond or Petersburg, Virginia, except a few angry looks from white bystanders.

On May 5 the buses pulled into Farmville, where the Justice Department under Attorney General Kennedy had filed suit against the county for transferring its public school property to white private schools. At the Farmville bus station, the Colored signs had been painted over. County authorities already had the fight over school integration to contend with and had evidently decided not to get involved in one over interstate bus station integration.

Nothing happened in Lynchburg, Virginia; but at the next stop, Danville, the riders were turned away by bus station officials. While they protested that they had a right to service, the riders decided not to insist, and no arrests were made.

On the morning of the following day, the Greyhound bus arrived at the Greyhound terminal in Rock Hill, South Carolina, where in February ten students sitting in at a McCrory's lunch counter were arrested and sentenced to either a $100 fine or thirty days' hard labor. Nine of the ten students chose to do the hard labor because their cause was just. The Rock Hill Jail-In, as it came to be called, was an early example of the willingness of students to do whatever was necessary in the nonviolent struggle for their rights.

It was also an early example of the willingness of students in the SNCC to show unity with fellow students by putting their own lives on the line. Four students—Diane Nash from Nashville, Tennessee; Charles Sherrod from Petersburg, Virginia; Charles Jones from Charlotte, North Carolina; and Ruby Doris from Atlanta, Georgia—had volunteered to go to Rock Hill and sit in, be arrested, and refuse bail just as the ten Rock Hill students had done. They served a thirty-two day sentence. Many in SNCC later marked Rock Hill as the real beginning of SNCC because of the way it involved the organization with a local grassroots movement.

The jail-in meant so much to young Freedom Rider and SNCC member John Lewis that he made a point of being the first in the line of Freedom Riders to enter the Rock Hill terminal. His way was blocked by several white youths who were hanging out at the terminal's pinball machines. First they shoved him, then one punched him in the jaw, knocking him to the ground. Several proceeded to kick him. Freedom Rider Albert Bigelow was behind Lewis and stepped between Lewis and his attackers. He was promptly knocked down, and as fists flew, Genevieve Hughes, who was in line behind Bigelow, was knocked down as well.

Police arrived to break up the attack and drag Lewis and Bigelow, bleeding but conscious, to safety. The police captain wanted Lewis and Bigelow to press charges against the white youths, whom he evidently regarded as troublemakers; but Lewis and Bigelow explained that to do so was not in the spirit of nonviolent resistance. Disgusted, the captain waved them into the terminal, where all the Freedom Riders were served the food they ordered.

Two hours later, when the Trailways bus arrived, the terminal was closed and locked. At a meeting that evening at Friendship Junior College, the Freedom Riders on the second bus heard a full report on what had happened to the other riders. John Lewis was the hero of the evening. Then he received an urgent message that he was a finalist in a competition for a grant to live and work in India among followers of Mohandas Gandhi. He had to travel to Philadelphia immediately for a personal interview. Regretfully, the next morning he left the Freedom Riders, who would go south without him toward Columbia, South Carolina, and Augusta, Georgia.

The Freedom Riders' singing was more lusty and heartfelt as they continued on their journey, for now they were afraid, and the words in songs such as "We Shall Overcome" gave them some comfort.

We shall overcome, we shall overcome
We shall overcome, some day
Oh, deep in my heart, I do believe
That we shall overcome some day.

We are not afraid, we are not afraid
We are not afraid today
Oh, deep in my heart, I do believe
That we shall overcome some day.

They arrived in Atlanta, Georgia, on May 13, without further incident and having traveled almost seven hundred miles. They celebrated this victory at an evening dinner that was attended by Dr. Martin Luther King, Jr. King praised their courage in completing that portion of their journey and their determination to continue on into the Deep South. He did not publicly express his misgivings about the dangers that lay ahead of them. But he took *Jet* reporter Simeon Booker aside and warned, "You will never make it through Alabama."[2] In response, Booker joked that his plan was to stay close to Farmer. The heavyset CORE executive director couldn't run very fast, and any white attacker would get Farmer first.

But that night Farmer received a telephone call that would change his plans as a Freedom Rider. Back in Washington, D.C, his father had died in his hospital bed after a long illness. The elder man had kept a copy of the Freedom Riders' itinerary, and Mrs. Farmer would later say that she was certain her husband had chosen to die just before his son entered Alabama. With a sense of relief that made him feel guilty, Farmer took leave of the group and returned to Washington for his father's funeral.

The remaining Freedom Riders chose to continue without Farmer. A few students had joined the group in Atlanta, and Joseph Perkins, a student from Michigan, took over Farmer's position as group captain on the Greyhound bus. James Peck took that job on the Trailways bus as both buses headed west out of Atlanta on U.S. Highway 78. Also on the buses were investigators from the state of Alabama dressed in plainclothes and scattered anonymously among the other passengers.

The Greyhound bus stopped in Tallapoosa, Georgia, and Heflin, Alabama, where drivers heading east told the driver that a large mob was massing at the next stop, Anniston, Alabama. When the driver in turn told Joseph Perkins, he was not surprised. CORE staffers had scouted some of the locations ahead of time, and Anniston had been identified as a potential trouble spot. The Freedom Riders were wary as the bus pulled into the Anniston bus terminal and frightened when they saw a large group of white men armed with baseball bats, bricks, and knives. When the driver turned off the engine, the nine Freedom Riders and five other passengers made no move to get out.

The mob shouted for the Freedom Riders to come out. Then they tried to force open the door. The two Alabama investigators in plainclothes rushed to the door and braced themselves against it. The angry mob then used their weapons against the bus, bashing at its sides with their clubs and slashing at the tires with their knives. The frightened passengers pleaded with the driver to leave the depot before the bus was disabled, and the driver needed no convincing. As the bus eased through the mob, Anniston police suddenly appeared to direct the bus out of town. They had been nowhere in sight during the attack.

As the bus sped along Highway 78 toward Birmingham,

about fifty cars filled with white hoodlums formed an ominous parade behind it. Inside, the terrified passengers wondered what was in the minds of their two-hundred-odd pursuers. Would they try to overtake the bus? Or were they just functioning as an escort, making sure the bus left town?

Their questions were answered soon, for not long after the bus left Anniston, the slashed tires of the vehicle began to lose air, and the bus listed to one side as some of its tires started to go flat. The frightened driver pulled off to the side of the highway, brought the bus to a stop, and fled, leaving the horrified passengers at the mercy of the pursuing mob.

The hoodlums swarmed out of their cars and attacked the disabled bus, smashing the windows, ripping open the baggage compartments, and prying open the door. Then a firebomb crashed through the smashed back window, and as flames engulfed the bus, the passengers tried to get out the door. But now the mob outside was barricading the door to keep the passengers inside. One of the Alabama investigators on board the bus went to the door, pulled his gun, and waved it at the mob, which fell back. Panic-stricken Freedom Riders tumbled out of the bus, only to be clubbed and beaten by the waiting mob.

The burning bus was in the yard of the Forsyths, a white family in Anniston. Twelve-year-old Janie Forsyth watched in horror as the bus went up in flames and as dazed Freedom Riders stumbled into the yard and fell to the grass. Janie wanted to do something, so she began to take water to the Freedom Riders, much to the displeasure of white onlookers. But to the young girl, it didn't matter who the injured were; they were people who needed help.

Finally, a contingent of Alabama state troopers arrived at the scene. They fired warning shots above the crowd, causing the attackers to disperse. The troopers then took the wounded passengers to Anniston Hospital.

The Freedom Riders on the Trailways bus had stopped in different towns and had no idea what had happened in Anniston. When their bus arrived in Anniston about an hour later, they wondered about the nervousness of the white onlookers as they entered the whites-only restaurant at the terminal, ordered sandwiches, and were served. Meanwhile, the bus driver had whispered conversations with some Anniston police officers and some bystanders. When the riders reboarded the bus with their sandwiches, the driver came back with about eight white men. He announced to the passengers, "We have received word that a bus has been burned to the ground and passengers are being carried to the hospital by the carloads. A mob is waiting for our bus and will do the same to us unless we get these niggers off the front seats."[3]

After a silence, while the individual Freedom Riders thought about what was in store for them and what they should do, one spoke up with the usual response, "We are interstate passengers with the right to sit anywhere on the bus." He had not even finished speaking when one of the whites with the driver slammed his fist into the face of Charles Person, a freshman at Morehouse College who was in the front seat of the bus. Another white hoodlum reached over and hit Morris Brown College sophomore Herbert Harris. The two white men then dragged the students into the aisle and continued to beat them.

Two white Freedom Riders came forward from the back of the bus to protest. James Peck, the group captain on the bus, took a blow that knocked him over two seat backs. Walter Bergman, the retired professor from Michigan, took a fist that knocked him to the floor. The white hoodlums continued to beat the two white Freedom

Riders. An anguished cry came from Mrs. Bergman, seated in the rear, "Don't beat him anymore! He's my husband!"

The attackers returned to their first two victims, dragged them down the aisle to the back of the bus, and threw them into the backseats. They threw Peck back there as well. Then they sat down in the middle seats to make sure no black passengers could move up front.

The bus driver had disappeared during the attacks. He now returned with a policeman, who surveyed the scene and left. The driver then revved the motor and took off along back roads, hoping to avoid the mob that was waiting on the highway to Birmingham. The beaten and bleeding Freedom Riders sprawled across the back-seats moaned with pain at every bump in the road.

All of Birmingham seemed to be waiting for the Freedom Ride buses. The Reverend Fred Shuttlesworth, one of the founders, with Martin Luther King, Jr., of the SCLC, had heard rumors that the local Ku Klux Klan planned to attack the Freedom Riders at the bus terminal there. An FBI informant who had infiltrated the Klan told the bureau that Birmingham police had agreed to give the Klan fifteen minutes of attack time before moving in.

Local reporters had also heard the rumors and made plans to cover the arrival of the first bus, due in at the Greyhound terminal. Howard K. Smith, a commentator for CBS, was passing through Birmingham on his way to New York. On hearing the rumors, he too made his way to the Greyhound depot.

Then the FBI informant learned from the police that the Trailways bus was going to arrive first. He told his Klan friends, who hightailed it to the Trailways terminal four blocks away. The reporters quickly followed.

The Trailways bus pulled into the Birmingham terminal.

Immediately, the eight men who had boarded at Anniston and beaten up the four Freedom Riders left the bus and disappeared into the crowd. James Peck and Charles Person painfully rose from their seats. They were the designated testers for Birmingham and were supposed to leave the bus first. Peck, his face and shirt caked with blood, stepped from the bus, with Person right behind him. The sight of the menacing mob was frightening, and they looked at each other for a moment. Then they started for the waiting room.

As they pushed through the crowded corridor, Peck overheard someone mutter that they should kill Person, because he must have been the one to hurt the white man, Peck. Several men started for Person, but Peck told them not to hurt him. The idea of a white man defending a black infuriated the crowd, which started to push Person toward the Negro waiting room and then began to hit him. Peck tried to help Person and was himself knocked down. The mob then set upon the two men with fists, feet, metal pipes, and clubs.

When they saw what was happening to Person and Peck, the Freedom Riders behind them tried to escape, but Klansmen blocked their path, then proceeded to beat them as well. In the melee, innocent bystanders, white and black, were hurt as they unsuspectingly entered the terminal or emerged from the rest rooms. A white photographer from the Birmingham *Post-Herald* took pictures of the attack on Peck, then faced the fury of the mob. He was clubbed and his camera smashed. Before he lost the camera, the photographer managed to remove the film.

The news director for WAPI News was in his car outside the terminal reporting on the scene on his car radio. Seeing him speaking into a microphone, members of the mob smashed the car windows, dragged the man out of the car onto the street, and ripped off his microphone.

All this violence took place in the space of about fifteen minutes. At the end of that previously agreed-upon time, Birmingham police arrived, just as the triumphant Klansmen were getting into their cars and leaving the scene.

Simeon Booker, the reporter for *Jet,* had escaped in a Negro taxi and made his way to the home of the Reverend Fred Shuttlesworth. On hearing Booker's reports of the attacks on the Freedom Riders, Shuttlesworth began to organize volunteer rescue squads. But before the first squad set out, Negro taxis began to arrive with broken and bleeding Freedom Riders. Charles Person, his head bleeding from many cuts, arrived before James Peck, his face covered with blood and several teeth broken. Seeing Person, Peck staggered over to him to shake his hand. Then the two men were put in private cars bound for the closest Negro and white hospitals.

James Peck was refused admittance to Carraway Methodist Hospital, which wanted no trouble with mobs. He was accepted at Hillman Hospital, where doctors used fifty-three stitches to close the six wounds to his head that he had received in both Anniston and Birmingham. As photographers snapped pictures, reporters fired questions at him. Although weak, Peck answered all questions and astonished his listeners when he insisted he would be on the bus the next day, headed for Montgomery.

Barely had Persons and Peck been taken away when Shuttlesworth received a call for help from Anniston Hospital, where Freedom Riders from the burned Greyhound had been taken. Members of the mob had followed them, and the frightened hospital personnel had refused to treat them. Unwanted, but afraid to leave, they were trapped.

Shuttlesworth organized a rescue mission, intending to lead it himself. But his volunteer drivers didn't think much of his insis-

1961, New York, New York. Two Freedom Riders publicize their cause: James Peck protests his beating and Henry Thomas protests his arrest outside the Trailways bus terminal in New York City's Port Authority.

tence that there be no guns allowed in the rescue cars. After convincing him that he was too valuable at his command post, the volunteers set out on the sixty-mile drive to Anniston, heavily armed. They rescued the Freedom Riders and delivered them to Birmingham hospitals without incident.

The violence in Anniston and Birmingham was headline news across the nation—on radio and television news that night and in newspaper headlines the following morning. It was not just a local story but a national and international one. Howard K. Smith, the CBS radio commentator, wrote an eyewitness account for the front page of the *New York Times*. The *Washington Post* ran a photograph of the burning Greyhound bus on its front page. James Farmer saw it and had an idea for a symbol for the Freedom Rides: the burning bus superimposed over the Statue of Liberty. His father's funeral was over, but Farmer had much yet to do to straighten out the elder man's affairs. He could not rejoin the Freedom Rides and was secretly relieved.

Attorney General Robert F. Kennedy read the headline stories and called Shuttlesworth's home. Shuttlesworth asked for protection for the Freedom Riders. Kennedy then put in a call to Alabama governor John Patterson to see what he could do about protecting riders.

The Birmingham *Post-Herald* photographer had managed to save his film from the mob at the bus depot. Some of his pictures were carried in newspapers in Tokyo, Japan, where the new president of the Birmingham Chamber of Commerce was attending an international business convention. He had hoped to attract more Japanese business to his city and was furious at the violent images of Birmingham displayed on the front pages of the Tokyo newspapers. He was embarrassed at the stares and questions from the

Japanese, who immediately lost interest in doing business in Birmingham.

In Nashville, Tennessee, the students involved in the local sit-in campaign questioned John Lewis, who had stopped there on his way back from his interview in Philadelphia to rejoin the Freedom Ride. Diane Nash, one of the leaders of the sit-ins, urged that a contingent of Nashville students go to Birmingham and join the Freedom Rides. She called Farmer to ask if it would be all right. Farmer gave Nash his assent, although he found it hard to imagine why the students would so willingly put their lives on the line.

Meanwhile, the eighteen Freedom Riders had decided they'd had enough. The original plan was to arrive in New Orleans, Louisiana, on May 17, the seventh anniversary of the Supreme Court's *Brown* decision. The bus burning and beatings had put them off schedule. They decided to get out of Birmingham, forget Montgomery, and fly directly to New Orleans. But as they left the bus terminal for the airport, a group of hoodlums pursued them and overtook them, reaching the airport before they did. Soon, a series of bomb threats prevented the departure of all planes scheduled to leave Birmingham for New Orleans.

Robert Kennedy's aide John Seigenthaler arrived at the Birmingham airport and concocted a plan to get the Freedom Riders off the ground. Airport personnel were instructed not to answer the telephone until the Freedom Riders had boarded the next plane for New Orleans and were safely off the ground. At last the eighteen frightened, wounded people were able to escape. But the Freedom Ride was not over. In Nashville, Diane Nash announced that a group of students were going to Birmingham, determined to take over the bus trip the CORE group had abandoned.

CHAPTER SEVEN

THE FREEDOM RIDES CONTINUE

The Reverend James Bevel of Nashville had selected ten volunteers, for the students had raised enough money for ten interstate bus tickets. Bevel chose John Lewis because he had started with the CORE group of Freedom Riders. He also chose five other black male students, two black females, one white male, and one white female, all of whom he believed would stick to the nonviolent principles of the sit-in campaigns. He did not choose Diane Nash, because he felt she was too valuable as a leader of the student movement there. He did not select himself, he explained to the others, because he had promised to drive to New York with some furniture for a friend.

The Nashville student volunteers knew what might be in store for them. Some wrote out their wills or said good-bye to their parents before they left Nashville on a Greyhound bus. To avoid trouble, they had decided that whites and blacks would not sit together. But once on the bus, two male students, one white and one black, insisted on sitting beside each other.

Some two hundred miles outside Nashville, the bus—with its Freedom Rider passengers heartily singing freedom songs—approached the Birmingham city limits, where it was flagged down by Birmingham police. Several officers boarded and immediately

53

arrested the integrated twosome, as other officers in patrol cars escorted the bus to the terminal. On arrival, more officers boarded the bus, taped newspapers over the windows, and then checked the passengers who wished to debark. Everyone whose ticket was for travel between Nashville and New Orleans was told to stay on the bus. Anyone who protested was pushed back into the seat. But one Freedom Rider, Selyn McCollum, had missed the bus out of Nashville and boarded instead at Pulaski, Tennessee, so the police didn't know she was a Freedom Rider. She left the bus, quickly found a telephone, and called Diane Nash in Nashville to report that the students were trapped on the Greyhound. Nash then called the Justice Department.

After about an hour, the Birmingham police officers guarding the bus received orders from headquarters to let the Freedom Riders leave the bus and enter the terminal. The students walked single file through a corridor formed by police to protect them from an angry, jeering white crowd. Once the students were inside the terminal, the police suggested they not enter the white waiting room in integrated groups. But the students were well versed in the *Boynton* decision and insisted on their right to do so.

They waited three hours in the white waiting room for the bus to Montgomery. Every time the mob moved toward them, the police pushed the crowd back, causing many in the crowd to turn their anger against the police. Then, just as the nine Nashville Freedom Riders were about to board the bus to Montgomery, Birmingham sheriff Eugene "Bull" Connor arrived and arrested them. He told reporters nearby that he was putting them under "protective custody," which was true. No authority in Alabama was prepared to guarantee the safety of the Freedom Riders in that state, and plenty of ordinary citizens were prepared to guarantee that the

Nashville students never left the state in one piece. Meanwhile, President John F. Kennedy and his brother Attorney General Robert Kennedy were loath to send federal troops in, fearing the reaction of southern states, whose leaders and citizens fervently guarded their states' rights against the encroachment of federal power.

In the Birmingham jail, the SNCC students refused to eat and sang freedom songs until their jailers covered their ears with their hands in protest. Sheriff Connor knew he couldn't keep them in jail, for they had done nothing illegal. So that night the students were dragged from the jail into police cars, which then drove off into the night. The frightened students wondered if they would be delivered to the Ku Klux Klan, never to be heard from again. Finally, after about a hundred miles, the police caravan stopped and the students were unceremoniously deposited, with their luggage, at a railroad track in the middle of nowhere. Only later did they learn that they had been dumped just across the Alabama-Tennessee state line and thus were no longer the responsibility of Alabama authorities.

There were only seven of them now, the other two having been bailed out of the Birmingham jail by their parents. They found a pay phone and called a surprised Diane Nash, who had already sent eleven more student volunteers off to Birmingham.

The stranded students found refuge in the home of a black couple and discussed their situation. They did not want to go back to Nashville, because to do so would be allowing the Alabama segregationists to win. They called Nash again to inform her that they wanted to go back to Alabama. Nash found a volunteer driver, who took off almost immediately on the hundred-mile journey to Ardmore, Tennessee, and the stranded students.

As Sheriff Bull Connor celebrated his victory over the Nashville Freedom Riders, radio reports began to come in that reinforcements were on the way from Nashville *and* that the original students were heading back to Birmingham by car. Hearing these same reports over the radio in the car that was taking them back to Birmingham, John Lewis and his six cohorts became terrified that the Ku Klux Klan would ambush them somewhere on the highway. They quickly lay down on the floor and backseat of the car, stacked on top of each other, afraid even to have the windows open for fear of sniper fire. The driver decided to leave the highway and take back roads instead, causing the students even more discomfort as the car drove over the bumpy back roads.

Reaching Birmingham safely, the driver went immediately to the home of Fred Shuttlesworth, where the eleven reinforcements were waiting. Then the entire group headed for the Greyhound terminal and the five o'clock bus to Montgomery in a third attempt to proceed with the original Freedom Rides schedule.

At the terminal, a Greyhound official told them that the scheduled bus to Montgomery had been canceled for lack of a driver. The Nashville students announced that they were prepared to wait however long it took for a bus to Montgomery. Meanwhile, Birmingham police estimated the crowd of angry segregationists at the terminal to be at least three thousand; police canine units were brought in to help keep the mob back. Frustrated crowd members could do nothing but throw rocks over the heads of the cordon of police officers.

In Washington, D.C., President Kennedy tried to reach Alabama governor John Patterson, but Patterson refused to take the president's call. He would only speak face-to-face with a representative of the president. John Seigenthaler took off by car from Birmingham to the state capitol in Montgomery. During Seigenthaler's meeting with the governor, Patterson declared that Alabama could protect the Freedom Riders without federal help. Meanwhile, attorneys for the state secured an injunction addressed to James Farmer and CORE forbidding "the entry into and travel within the state of Alabama, and engaging in the so-called 'Freedom Ride' and other acts or conduct calculated to promote breaches of the peace." Although neither Farmer nor any other members of CORE were with the Nashville students, the injunction would soon be used as a reason to arrest them.

The next day, Saturday, May 20, dawned in Birmingham, and still no Greyhound bus driver was willing to pilot a bus to Montgomery. Finally, after negotiations with the head of the bus drivers union, a driver was found. At 8:30 A.M. the St. Petersburg Express set off for Montgomery with John Lewis and the other Nashville students aboard. They had waited six days to make their bus connection in Birmingham. The high-speed trip was uneventful, and the bus arrived in Montgomery a half hour ahead of schedule.

John Lewis stepped off the bus first, followed by the others. Lewis had expected the group of reporters. He had not expected the terminal to be practically deserted otherwise. Except for a few drivers parked in their taxis and about a dozen white men at the terminal entrance, the terminal area was empty. Lewis didn't like it.

He had just begun to deliver his statement to the press when he saw the crowd of white men advancing, armed with lead pipes, bottles, and baseball bats. One of the men slapped a reporter from NBC News, and then the others attacked the reporters, smashing cameras and microphones.

"Let's all stand together!" cried Lewis as hoodlums slammed into the group of Freedom Riders and forced them over a railing into the parking lot below. There, other whites who had been hiding emerged from behind doorways and posts. Some of the terrified Freedom Riders jumped into several Negro taxis and screamed to the drivers to take them to a nearby church. But mobs blocked the parking lot exits. One taxi driver abandoned his vehicle, leaving his passengers to the mob's fury.

Thugs set upon Jim Zwerg, a white student from Wisconsin who was attending the black Fisk University in Nashville. They smashed his suitcase into his face to knock him down, then some pinned him to the ground as others knocked out his teeth with their fists. Susan Wilbur, a white student, was dragged out of a Negro taxi and set upon by white women who beat at her with their pocketbooks.

There were no police in evidence. John Seigenthaler of the Justice Department drove up to the terminal in his car, believing that the Greyhound had not yet arrived. He saw the attack on Susan Wilbur and decided to try to rescue her. He drove up to the curb and jumped out just as a heavy blow from one of the women sent her flying across the bumper of his car. He pulled her into the front

1961, Montgomery, Alabama. James Zwerg of Nashville, Tennessee (left), with John Lewis of Troy, Alabama (right), after they were attacked and beaten when their Greyhound bus arrived in Montgomery.

seat as the women continued to pound at her with their purses.

Wilbur screamed at him, "Mister, this is not your fight! away from here! You're gonna get killed!" Moments later, a lead pipe blow to his head knocked Seigenthaler unconscious.

Wilbur and the other white female student, Susan Harmon, managed to flee to a nearby church. Montgomery police put them on a train back to Nashville. The students in the abandoned Negro taxi managed to escape to a black home. Others had found refuge in scattered places throughout the city.

Back at the terminal, three Freedom Riders lay unconscious, some in pools of their own blood. The crowd of angry whites numbered close to one thousand. By the time Montgomery police commissioner L. B. Sullivan arrived with a force of cops, the violence was over. Alabama attorney general MacDonald Gallion was with Sullivan. Directed by someone to the unconscious John Lewis, who had been smashed in the head with a soda crate, Gallion stood over Lewis's body and began to read the injunction against the Freedom Riders.

Lewis roused and struggled to his feet. He found and revived his seminary schoolmate, William Barbie, and the white exchange student Jim Zwerg. Zwerg was in bad shape, but under Alabama's segregation laws no Negro taxi or ambulance could transport a white person; and all the ambulances for whites were mysteriously out of commission. At last, the police allowed a Negro ambulance to take Zwerg to a local Catholic hospital that had agreed to accept him.

Released from the hospital, Lewis went to the home of the Reverend S. S. Seay, where the scattered Freedom Riders had regrouped. While they had been through a harrowing experience, they were triumphant. Diane Nash, in constant touch by telephone, had excitedly told them that the story was big. President Kennedy's personal representative had been beaten up at the terminal. Reporters from the major newspapers were on their way to Montgomery to cover the story. She was going to Montgomery herself, and Martin Luther King, Jr., might come, too.

William Barbie's and Jim Zwerg's wounds were serious enough to keep them hospitalized. From their beds, both told reporters that they were prepared to die, if necessary, in order to complete their journey. As for Seigenthaler, he was also in the hospital in serious condition, and in Washington, Attorney General Kennedy was again threatening federal intervention.

Also in the nation's capital, James Farmer was concerned that the Nashville students were taking control of CORE's Freedom Ride campaign. He ordered his staff in New York to recruit a contingent of CORE Freedom Riders to go to Alabama.

Meanwhile, the Nashville Freedom Riders were in hiding, for if found, they faced certain arrest under the special anti–Freedom Rider injunction. Their hiding place on May 21 was the basement of the First Baptist Church, whose pastor was the Reverend Ralph David Abernathy, Martin Luther King, Jr.'s closest aide and friend.

Around noon that day, King flew into Montgomery. He was escorted by federal marshals to Abernathy's home, where the two old friends made plans for a mass meeting at Abernathy's church that night. Diane Nash arrived in Montgomery and also went to Abernathy's. James Farmer was due in that night.

Word got out about the mass meeting, and by the time latecomers had arrived they were reporting that they had to dodge rocks hurled by a growing crowd of whites who were daring the blacks inside the church to come out. As the night wore on, the crowd outside grew braver. Firebombs were thrown; a car was overturned and burned. Federal marshals were spread too thinly to contain a massive outbreak of violence. Inside, anxious telephone calls to the attorney general's office resulted in telephone negotiations between Washington and Alabama governor Patterson. At last, Patterson agreed to proclaim a state of martial law, and the Alabama National Guard moved in with tear gas to control the crowd.

The church windows, open for ventilation on the warm May night, had to be closed for safety. The people inside the church were hot and beginning to have a trapped feeling.

Indeed, they were trapped. When some in the church tried to leave, they were not allowed to do so. When a few began to push their way through the guardsmen, they were forced back with rifle butts. Instead of feeling protected, the audience felt like prisoners. King and others calmed the crowd and made arrangements for the hundreds of people inside the church to spend the night there, giving the cushioned pews to children and old people, organizing lines for the one small bathroom and the single telephone. Not until 4:30 the following morning did the first groups leave the church in National Guard trucks. The following day, a curfew was imposed, and jeeps patrolled the streets.

The siege over, the civil rights leaders assembled in Montgomery turned their thoughts again to the continuation of the Freedom Rides. Diane Nash pressured King to join a ride, but he steadfastly refused. The Freedom Rides had proved violent beyond any of their imaginings, and he feared for his personal safety. Moreover, his aides insisted that he was too valuable a spokesman for the movement. Besides, he was on probation from a 1960 arrest on a trumped-up traffic charge in Georgia, and if arrested as a Freedom Rider, as he surely would be, he faced six months in a Georgia prison.

The thoughts of Robert Kennedy and his aides in

Washington, D.C., also returned to the matter of the Freedom Rides. The attorney general did not want to anger the South by having federal marshals escort the Freedom Riders to Mississippi, but he did not trust either Alabama or Mississippi to protect the Freedom Riders. In the end, he agreed to allow such injunctions as had been handed down against the Freedom Riders in Alabama to stand, even though the injunctions were unconstitutional. He would let state officials arrest the Freedom Riders rather than see them beaten or killed by segregationist mobs. According to a carefully worked-out plan, the Freedom Riders would travel under heavy escort between Montgomery and Jackson, Mississippi, where they would be arrested. Neither CORE nor the Freedom Riders were informed of the plan.

The Freedom Riders prepared to continue their journey. Their decision was to go on as before, with one group on a Trailways bus and the other on a Greyhound. There were enough volunteers to ride the two buses. A carload of students from Nashville would take part, as well as a group of sit-in veterans from Washington, D.C. This latter group included Howard University students Stokely Carmichael, William Mahoney, and John Moody, and a white divinity student named Paul Dietrich. Five CORE volunteers had also arrived from New Orleans, but while James Farmer was anxious to reestablish his organization's control of the Freedom Rides, he had decided not to go himself.

Having been away attending to his father's funeral and estate for four weeks, Farmer argued that his CORE desk in New York was piled high with mail. The publicity surrounding the Freedom Rides had catapulted his small organization into national prominence, and he wanted to take advantage of it to raise money and membership. But, like King, he was mostly afraid for his own personal safety. As he later wrote, "Frankly, I was scared spitless and desperately wanted to avoid taking that ride to Jackson."[1]

Early on Wednesday morning, cars of Freedom Riders and civil rights leaders made their way under heavy Alabama National Guard truck escort to the Trailways bus station in downtown Montgomery. To show their support, King and other leaders of his organization, the SCLC, led the group into the white waiting room and ordered coffee. Promptly waited on, they were the first blacks ever to receive such service. Then the Freedom Riders went outside to the loading platform and were surprised to see soldiers guarding the seven o'clock bus and turning away all other passengers. Only Freedom Riders and reporters were allowed on board. A wave of nervousness swept through the group as they wondered what lay ahead of them. Thoughts of an ambush on the highway crossed many minds. They knew from experience that having reporters with them offered no protection, for angry white mobs had already beaten reporters and smashed their equipment for daring to cover the Freedom Rides.

Some volunteers changed their minds, and only twelve Freedom Riders, nearly all of them Nashville students, actually boarded the bus. Sixteen reporters did so as well. Then, suddenly, twelve National Guardsmen got on, carrying bayoneted rifles and announcing that they were there to protect the Freedom Riders.

Motorcycle policemen escorted the Trailways bus to the city limits, where escort duties were taken over by dozens of highway patrol cars, helicopters, and U.S. Border Patrol airplanes. Governor Patterson had determined to show every African American alive that the only way to travel through Alabama in an integrated group was with this type of unprecedented security.

Inside the bus, the Freedom Riders and reporters were

informed that all stops between Montgomery and Jackson had been canceled, and the bus began to travel at speeds of up to 70 MPH on what was usually a seven-hour trip.

When the high-speed caravan stopped at the Mississippi line to allow Mississippi National Guardsmen to take over, the Reverend James Lawson, a young black Baptist minister from Nashville, protested the enormous military escort as going against the philosophy of the Freedom Rides. "We would rather risk violence and be able to travel like ordinary passengers," he told reporters, adding, "We will accept the violence and the hate, absorb it without returning it."[2] The reporters thought he was crazy. Like the Freedom Riders, the reporters did not know of the state and federal plans to deliver the Freedom Riders safely to their arrests in Jackson.

What state and federal officials did not know was that there was a second group of Freedom Riders planning to leave Montgomery later that morning. When word came that fourteen Freedom Riders had bought tickets on the 11:25 A.M. Greyhound bus out of Montgomery, Attorney General Robert F. Kennedy was furious. So were Mississippi and Alabama authorities. The Alabama escort had just started back from taking the Trailways bus to the Mississippi line. No similar military escort could be quickly arranged for the Greyhound bus. The attorney general angrily announced that no federal marshals would accompany the Greyhound and that this second busload had "nothing to do with the Freedom Rides."

At the Greyhound terminal, Alabama National Guardsmen used their bayonets to hold back a swelling crowd of angry whites who frightened the fourteen Freedom Riders. Then news came of Kennedy's statements. Even in their fear, they saw the irony of his words: This contingent had CORE volunteers, including two students from New Orleans named Jerome Smith and Doris Castle, and Henry Thomas, who had been on the bus that had been burned in Anniston. They had everything to do with the Freedom Rides. And from all reports, it seemed that this group of Freedom Riders might be in as much danger as those who had gone to Anniston.

James Farmer was aware of the danger as he escorted the group to the Greyhound bus. After watching the volunteers board and take seats, he walked along the outside of the bus, shaking hands with his troops through the windows. When he reached the window where Doris Castle was sitting, he smiled and offered his hand, saying, "My prayers are with you, Doris. Have a safe trip, and when it's over, we'll get together and decide what we have to do next to finish the job."

The young woman's eyes widened in fear. "You're coming with us, aren't you Jim," she whispered urgently.

Farmer started to explain again all the reasons why he had to return to CORE headquarters, but the girl just shook her head slowly. "Jim, *please!*" she pleaded, and Farmer realized that he could not let her go alone. He, too, boarded the bus.[3]

In addition to the Freedom Riders, six reporters and six Alabama National Guardsmen boarded the bus. As the bus pulled out of the depot, reserve helicopters hastily called into service moved in to precede the bus, scanning the highway and the woods ahead for any sign of trouble. In spite of their anger over the unexpected second Freedom Ride out of Montgomery, state and federal officials had decided that they had better treat this bus as a Freedom Ride bus after all.

Not long after the Greyhound had departed, another Greyhound bus arrived in Montgomery. An interracial group of

nine men were on it, including Charles Jones, a member of SNCC;
two English professors from Wesleyan University; and two clergymen from Yale University, including the university's chaplain, the
Reverend William Sloane Coffin, Jr. They had started their trip in
Atlanta, Georgia, and had been testing small-town bus facilities at
every stop between there and Montgomery.

This was just too much for state and federal authorities. The
Freedom Rides had become like small brushfires that kept igniting
every time the officials thought they had stamped them out. And
this latest group was not composed of student rabble-rousers but
professors from Ivy League colleges. Attorney General Robert
Kennedy pleaded for a "cooling-off period," warning other would-
be Freedom Riders to delay their trips.

The crowd at the Montgomery Greyhound terminal greeted
the newcomers with icy stares, then began hurling rocks and bottles
over the heads of the National Guardsmen who were keeping them
back. About twenty minutes later, two cars drove into a space
cleared by the guardsmen. The Reverend Ralph Abernathy jumped
out of his car and hurried the nine men into it. Packed in like sar-
dines, they were taken to Abernathy's house to meet with King and
to decide whether to continue on to Jackson.

Meanwhile, in Jackson, the Trailways bus arrived safely
with the first group of Freedom Riders, who had debarked and used
the whites-only rest-room facilities. Then they had been arrested by
Jackson police and taken to the city jail.

Several hundred miles away, the Greyhound bus did not stop
as scheduled in Selma, Alabama, due to reports of an angry white
mob, armed and waiting. At the Mississippi line, the driver left and
another took the seat behind the wheel. The Alabama National
Guardsmen turned their duties over to their Mississippi counter-

parts. All this was expected. But then an Alabama official whispered something to one of the reporters, and five of the six reporters soon left the bus.

As the Freedom Riders stared wide-eyed at the highway ahead of them, wondering when and where the ambush would come, the SNCC worker, Henry Thomas, began to sing:

1961, Jackson, Mississippi. John Lewis is arrested and taken to jail with 26 other Freedom Riders when their Greyhound bus arrives in Jackson.

I'm a takin' a ride
On the Greyhound bus line
I'm a-ridin' the *front seat*
To Jackson, this time.

Everyone joined in the chorus:

Hallelujah, I'm a-travelin'
Hallelujah, ain't it fine?
Hallelujah, I'm a-travelin'
Down freedom's main line.[4]

As the bus reached a heavily wooded area, the Freedom Riders saw Mississippi National Guardsmen on both sides of the highway, their rifles pointed into the woods. Clearly, this was the spot where the ambush was expected, but it did not come.

When the bus pulled into the Greyhound terminal in Jackson, a crowd of whites awaited the Freedom Riders. But as Farmer led his group toward the sea of white faces, it parted to let him through. This was no group of troublemakers; these were reporters, federal agents, and plainclothes police. Mississippi governor Ross Barnett had spent the day broadcasting over local radio and television airwaves asking the citizens of his state to stay at home and let the law take care of the Freedom Riders. His message had been heard and obeyed.

Farmer and his group entered the whites-only waiting room, drank from the whites-only water fountain, and then headed for the entrance to the whites-only restaurant. Their way was blocked by a police captain who asked them to move on. Farmer refused. The captain repeated his order two more times, and twice more Farmer refused, citing the Supreme Court decision in the *Boynton* case.

The Freedom Riders were then arrested and escorted to a police patrol wagon. As the paddy wagon headed for the city jail, the Freedom Riders sang "We Shall Overcome," saving their greatest lung power for the stanza that went

> We are not afraid, we are not afraid
> We are not afraid, today
> Oh, deep in my heart, I do believe
> We shall overcome, some day.

THE FREEDOM RIDERS IN JAIL

In the Jackson City Jail, the police processing the Freedom Riders—booking, fingerprinting, and taking mug shots of them—called them nigger and black bastard and boy. But they did not beat them. The Freedom Riders realized that they were being given special treatment, for it was customary for southern white police officers to beat prisoners—especially black prisoners. But the Freedom Riders were no ordinary prisoners. The eyes of the nation and the world were watching to see what happened to them.

As with everything else in Mississippi, the jails were segregated. The white Freedom Riders were put in separate cell blocks from the black Freedom Riders. But the two busloads of Freedom Riders amounted to more prisoners than the city jail could handle. That night the new prisoners were walked across the street to the Hinds County Jail, guarded by police officers standing shoulder to shoulder on both sides and armed with rifles in case anyone tried to shoot at them. But the only shooting of the Freedom Riders that night was done by still photographers and TV news cameramen who had taken up posts at the jail when the first Freedom Riders were brought in.

Again, they were segregated in the Hinds County Jail—

black men, black women, white men, white women. The sanitary facilities were inadequate, and the food was so bad that several of the students threatened to go on a hunger strike. They had no idea how long they would stay there or what lay in store for them. They kept up their spirits by singing.

Arrested in Jackson on May 24, the Freedom Riders came to trial on May 25. The trial was held quickly, and it was over just as quickly. The prosecuting attorney got up from his seat, accused them of trespassing, and returned to his seat. The attorneys for the Freedom Riders included Wiley Branton, an NAACP lawyer who had worked closely with Thurgood Marshall on many civil rights cases in the South and who had volunteered to defend the Freedom

1961, Baltimore, Maryland. During an attempted sit-in at a diner north of Baltimore, four of five Freedom Riders were jailed. At another diner, the proprietor had locked the doors against them.

Riders. CORE had also sent its own attorney, Jack Young. Both lawyers defended the Freedom Riders' rights as human beings. While they talked, the judge turned his back and looked at the wall behind him.

All the Freedom Riders pleaded guilty to violating Mississippi's segregation laws. All were convicted and sentenced to one year in jail. Under Mississippi law, one who had been convicted of a crime and could not or would not post bail had to spend forty days in jail before being eligible to file an appeal. SNCC and CORE urged all those who could do so to remain in jail for that length of time. The idea was to fill up the jails and place a great financial burden on the state of Mississippi. In fact, Farmer had asked his staff to keep Freedom Riders coming into Jackson on almost every bus, and SNCC was mobilizing its affiliates on campuses across the South.

This tactic was a new one for the civil rights movement. During the Montgomery bus boycott in 1955 and 1956 and in the later sit-in movement, demonstrators who were arrested were quickly bailed out of jail. The idea of packing jails was one borrowed from the Gandhi freedom movement in India. SNCC had first given voice to the policy in October 1960 when the Reverend James Lawson had cried in an impassioned speech, "Jail—No Bail." SNCC and CORE hoped this policy would have the same effect in Mississippi as it had in India—burdening the authorities and keeping the struggle uppermost in the minds of the people.

A few of the jailed Freedom Riders pleaded personal commitments and were bailed out. Most agreed to stay.

But being in jail was boring, and the food didn't get any better. Others began to approach Farmer to ask if they could be bailed out as well. Farmer agreed, but asked that the leave-taking be controlled—two Freedom Riders a day bailed out. Their places were taken by new Freedom Riders, arriving daily in Jackson.

The new prisoners did not include the group of university professors and clergymen from Connecticut. As previously planned, they had been accompanied by four black clergymen—Ralph Abernathy, Wyatt Tee Walker, Fred Shuttlesworth, and Bernard Lee—to the bus terminal's whites-only restaurant and been served. Then, Montgomery sheriff Mack Sim Butler had ordered all eleven men arrested. Seeing no point in staying in the Montgomery city jail, they had bailed themselves out.

In all, some twenty-seven Freedom Riders chose to remain in jail in Jackson. They were mostly male, and mostly college students. More than half were blacks. The whites were primarily Jews, including several rabbis.

Throughout the long days, they sang, knowing that it irritated their jailers. They did not realize that it also affected their fellow prisoners, who were mostly black. The Freedom Riders were kept segregated from the other prisoners. James Farmer wrote in his autobiography, *Lay Bare the Heart*, that one night a voice called down to them from the second floor: "Freedom Riders, if you teach us your songs, we'll teach you ours."[1] After that, the Freedom Riders learned work songs, protest songs, and gospel songs they had never heard before.

The jail guards were furious about this communication between the Freedom Riders and the other prisoners. As punishment, they told the Freedom Riders that they could no longer buy from the cart that was called "the store" and that sold candy, chips, chewing gum, cigarettes, and other items. But the Freedom Riders simply arranged for their upstairs friends to buy from the store for them. They would put money and a list of items they wanted in a handkerchief and tie that to a string lowered from an upstairs window. The items would later be delivered in the same manner.

Meanwhile, the Freedom Rides and the determination of many Freedom Riders to remain in jail excited the leaders of the civil rights movement. In Atlanta, Martin Luther King, Jr., led a meeting that resulted in the founding of the Freedom Ride Coordinating Committee. As Taylor Branch put it in his book *Parting the Waters,* "After an odyssey that had changed many lives and come to the attention of millions, they [the Freedom Riders and CORE] were allied formally with the heirs of the Montgomery bus boycott and the student sit-ins, maneuvering along a collision course with the federal government as well as the Southern states."[2]

James Farmer of CORE, Wyatt Tee Walker of the SCLC, and James Bevel and James Lawson of Nashville were represented by others at that meeting, since at the time all were in jail. SNCC did not have a leader, so it sent a representative. The six people vowed to end bus segregation in the South and to fill the jails in Montgomery and Jackson to keep the issue before the public. This was on May 26, just three weeks after the original CORE Freedom Riders had left Washington, D.C.

But the incredible press coverage, the riveted attention of the nation and the world, could not last forever. Southern authorities had shrewdly decided their own mobs of citizens were simply playing into the hands of the Freedom Riders with their violent response. There were no more bus burnings or beatings of Freedom Riders. Instead, every would-be Freedom Rider who arrived in the Deep South was arrested, and those willing to be reinforcements dwindled in number. After a while, they were primarily black politicians and clergymen from the North who flew down south to be arrested and then quickly bailed out.

Attorney General Robert Kennedy publicly criticized the Freedom Rides and warned against their continuation. Privately, he ordered his aides to meet with the various civil rights leaders to plan and coordinate a campaign to register thousands of black voters in the South, arguing that the best way to attack segregation was at the polling booth.

This idea was not new with Kennedy. It had been the original aim of the SCLC, and there were members of SNCC who believed that voting rights should be the chief aim of the civil rights movement. Other elements of SNCC, and of various older civil rights organizations, remained committed with religious fervor to the more confrontational direct-action tactics such as the Freedom Rides, which had brought such press attention to the movement.

About three weeks into the sentence of the first group of Freedom Riders to be arrested and jailed in Jackson, James Farmer was told by a black trusty (a prisoner who was trusted enough to do work around the jail) that the Freedom Riders were going to be transferred to the Hinds County Prison Farm. The prisoners upstairs warned the Freedom Riders that the farm was much worse than the in-town prison.

Farmer wondered about the reason for the move. He had learned from the attorney representing the Freedom Riders that the state of Mississippi had spent so much money on the Freedom Riders—adding to its police, investigation, and prison forces—that it could not go through with the planned elimination of some state taxes. And there was no end in sight. Perhaps, Farmer thought, the state would try to make their prison time so miserable that they would leave before the requisite forty days were over. Soon after arriving at Hinds County Prison Farm, Farmer decided that he was right.

Immediately on arrival, the Freedom Riders were met by the superintendent of the prison farm, who warned that singing would not be tolerated. They would be put into cells, the lights would be turned out, and they were not to make any noise at all. Breakfast would be served early and then each would be processed.

Whispering in the darkened cell block, the new prisoners agreed not to sing—at least not that first night. They wanted to wait and see what would happen the next day. Before leaving the county jail, Farmer had gotten a message to the group's attorney, asking him to bail out someone quickly so the world would know what was happening to them. He hoped the attorney would act quickly on that request.

Breakfast was served at six o'clock the following morning—the best breakfast they'd had since being arrested. But the quality of the food was the only good thing about Hinds County Prison Farm. One by one, they were taken to an interrogation room, questioned, and beaten.

Fortunately, after about an hour, the Freedom Riders' attorney arrived to bail out one of their number who had previously asked to be released. That Freedom Rider immediately called a press conference and then notified the FBI about what was happening to his fellows. Within two hours, FBI men had arrived, and that night the Freedom Riders were taken back to Jackson and the Hinds County Jail. There, a new group of Freedom Riders had been arrested and happily reported that the Freedom Rides were still front-page news. But that was the only good news for the imprisoned Freedom Riders. They soon learned that they were to be taken away again, this time to the Mississippi State Penitentiary in Parchman.

At the state penitentiary, the men and women were separated. Both groups were marched into large rooms and told to take all their clothes off. As prison guards laughed and pointed, the embarrassed prisoners struggled to keep their dignity. Then they were marched, naked, to their cells.

The men were taken to the prison's death row, which had been cleared out especially for them. The women were taken elsewhere in the prison. As new groups of Freedom Riders arrived, they were added to the same cell blocks, the whites and blacks only partially segregated. They were allowed no pencils or papers, no snacks or personal items. The food was worse than it had been at the Hinds County Jail, and they were given no opportunity to go out into the prison yard to exercise.

The Freedom Riders began to sing. As punishment, the guards took away the thin straw mattresses from their metal bunks. The Freedom Riders kept on singing. This time the guards doused them with a fire hose. Then they opened the windows and turned on powerful ceiling fans that drew chilling drafts over their bodies. By the next morning, many of the Freedom Riders had colds, but they kept singing.

Their meals from then on were so loaded with salt that they were barely edible. But they kept on singing. For the first Freedom Riders to be arrested, their forty days in jail were almost over. They knew they could hang on.

As James Farmer and the others in the first group climbed into the van that would take them back to Jackson and their freedom, another van arrived carrying newly arrested Freedom Riders. Up to that time, a total of 355 Freedom Riders had been arrested.

Back at CORE headquarters in New York, Farmer was pleased to see new volunteers arriving every day, and CORE chapters around the country were calling in to announce how many new recruits they could offer to the cause. It was July

1961, and the Freedom Rides were in their third month.

Calls for reinforcements swept across the nation's campuses. At Cornell University in Ithaca, New York, a math major named Bob Filner answered the call. He was just one of hundreds who initially signed up. But as the time to travel to the South on an interstate bus drew near, most of the eager recruits backed out. "We got to three days before we were going, and there were five of us," recalled Filner, who had become a city councilman in San Diego, California, in 1989. "And with a couple of days left, there were three of us. One kid, his father bought him a car if he wouldn't go. Finally, there were two of us left. . . . And when we finally got arrested, and the names got back to Cornell, they said 'Who's Bob Filner?'"[3]

After a few days of training in Nashville, Tennessee, and a daylong bus ride, Filner's group arrived in Jackson, Mississippi. By the time Filner was arrested in Jackson, he knew that every Freedom Rider who arrived was immediately arrested. But that did not make it any easier to face the mob of howling whites who continued to greet the buses. "If we hadn't been arrested, we would have been in real trouble," he remains convinced. "We would have been lynched."

Equally scary for Filner was being in Parchman Penitentiary. "Kids were beaten up. Kids were dragged around, and you were completely isolated from where we had started. Anything could happen to us. My mother kept writing to the warden, 'I hope you're taking care of my son.' He wrote back, 'Your son Robert is doing fine. He has had medical attention.' My family still has that letter from the warden."

The hardest thing about being in the prison for Filner was the boredom. The Freedom Riders could not have books, letters, or newspapers. They were allowed out of their cells just once a week to shower and receive a change of clothes. To keep from going crazy, Filner exercised. He did push-ups, sit-ups, and jumping jacks by the hour.

Filner was one of the youngest prisoners, and he believes that the warden thought that his youth might make him more vulnerable to psychological pressure. One day the warden called him into his office and told him, "You know what Martin Luther King is doing back in New York? He's driving around in a big car and eating good meals. And you're here. Don't you want to go home?" But Filner refused to play the warden's game.

The Freedom Rides finally ended when Attorney General Robert Kennedy succeeded in getting the Interstate Commerce Commission (ICC) to issue an order that he could enforce. In September, the ICC ordered that all For Colored and For White signs come down from the buses and terminal facilities used by interstate passengers. These signs were to be replaced by notices stating that segregation by race, color, creed, or national origin was unconstitutional and was an offense punishable by fine and/or imprisonment. The order was to go into effect on November 1, 1961, but the issuance of the order was enough for James Farmer. He told the attorney general that he was calling off the Freedom Rides. But on November 1, the date the order went into effect, he would send out interracial teams to crisscross the South and test the enforcement of the order. If it was not obeyed, he would resume the Freedom Rides immediately.

From time to time over the next several years, CORE, SNCC, and other organizations tested compliance with the FCC order, realizing that if they did not do so, they risked losing the fight that had already cost so much pain and suffering. In general, the order was obeyed, and when it was not, demonstrations resulted.

THE AFTERMATH OF THE FREEDOM RIDES

The Freedom Rides, following on the student sit-in movement, opened a new era of confrontation for the civil rights movement. The South became more resistant, and response to civil rights demonstrations became ever more violent.

In the fall of 1962 a young man named James Meredith attempted to enroll at the University of Mississippi. Governor Ross Barnett urged whites to "stand up like men and tell them, 'Never.'" Only after federal troops were sent in by President Kennedy and a riot broke out in which hundreds were injured and two died was Meredith finally registered.

In the spring of 1963, Martin Luther King, Jr., and the SCLC conducted a huge desegregation campaign in Birmingham, Alabama. The concept of nonviolence was sorely tested there as scores of demonstrators were beaten, poked with cattle prods, set upon with fire hoses and police dogs. Hundreds were jailed in Birmingham, including King himself.

The violent response to the civil rights movement continued in June 1963 when Medgar Evers, a field secretary for the NAACP, was shot and killed on his doorstep in Jackson, Mississippi.

That August, the leaders of all the major civil rights groups united to organize the March on Washington for Jobs and Freedom. It was the idea of A. Philip Randolph, an elder statesman of the civil rights movement who'd had a long career as a labor organizer and had founded the first black union, the Brotherhood of Sleeping Car Porters. The chief organizer of the march was Randolph's most trusted associate, Bayard Rustin. Rustin had taken part in the Journey of Reconciliation back in 1947.

The March on Washington was intended to pressure Congress to pass a civil rights bill that had been introduced by President Kennedy. The march attracted more than 250,000 peaceful demonstrators, black and white, old and young. They heard stirring speeches delivered from the steps of the Lincoln Memorial. Martin Luther King, Jr.'s "I Have a Dream" speech that day catapulted him to the forefront of civil rights movement leadership.

Unfortunately, the March on Washington represented the last time the leaders of the various civil rights organizations were united on anything. From that time on, they worked separately, pursuing different goals and jealously guarding their individual campaigns. Racist whites fought them all.

On September 15, 1963, a black church in Birmingham was bombed, killing four young girls. So many bombs went off in Birmingham that it earned the nickname Bombingham.

On November 22, 1963, President John F. Kennedy was assassinated while riding in a motorcade through the streets of Dallas, Texas. Many believed that the president had been killed because of his stand on civil rights. One of the first things Vice President Lyndon B. Johnson vowed to do after he succeeded to the presidency was to carry on President Kennedy's plans for civil rights laws.

SNCC, meanwhile, had decided to concentrate on a voter

registration campaign and declared the summer of 1964 to be Freedom Summer. In June, near Philadelphia, Mississippi, three SNCC volunteers—two young white men from New York, Andrew Goodman and Michael Schwerner, and a young black man from Mississippi, James Chaney—were beaten and shot and their bodies buried in a nearby dam. They did not live to witness the historic moment on July 2 when President Lyndon Johnson signed into law the Civil Rights Act of 1964. The most far-reaching civil rights legislation ever, it contained new provisions to help guarantee African Americans the right to vote and equal access to public accommodations.

1964, New York, New York. James Farmer, civil rights leader and national director of CORE, protests the lynching of Andrew Goodman, Michael Schwerner, and James Chaney. The three SNCC volunteers were killed outside Philadelphia, Mississippi, in June 1964.

White violence against SNCC workers in Alabama and Mississippi in the summer of 1964 caused SNCC to turn away from nonviolence as an effective tactic. But Martin Luther King, Jr., continued to believe that it was the only way to gain equal rights for one-tenth of the nation's people. In fact, in 1964 he was awarded the Nobel Prize for Peace for his continuing commitment to peaceful solutions to the problem of racial segregation in America. An international award, the Nobel Prize is highly respected. King was the youngest American, and only the second African American, to receive it.

In early 1965, King led a voter registration drive in Selma, Alabama. In late March, after Selma's whites reacted violently, King announced a march from Selma to the state's capital, Montgomery. The marchers were met by mounted state troopers and tear gas as they tried to cross the Edmund Pettus Bridge out of Selma. Many marchers, including Freedom Rides veteran John Lewis, were severely beaten on the day that became known forever after as Bloody Sunday.

Federal troops protected the marchers the rest of the way. But Viola Liuzzo, a white woman from Detroit who had volunteered to drive marchers back and forth, was shot and killed in her car by Ku Klux Klansmen.

In August 1965, President Johnson signed into law the Voting Rights Act, which strengthened the guarantees of African American voting rights.

Earlier that summer, blacks in the Watts section of Los Angeles had rioted. The civil rights scene shifted from the South to other regions. Movement leaders such as Martin Luther King, Jr., realized that they had neglected the black people outside the South. These people also suffered from racial discrimination. They were not segregated by law, but they were segregated in fact—in housing, in education, in jobs.

King decided to take his campaign north and attempted to organize nonviolent demonstrations in Chicago. But Chicago's blacks did not accept the principles of nonviolence. In fact, many African Americans no longer did. White violence had been too great, and there was much bitterness.

Within SNCC, disagreements over whether to continue the nonviolent course or to accept a policy of self-defense caused an irrevocable split. Many former SNCC members left to join more moderate organizations such as the SCLC. SNCC's new executive director, Stokely Carmichael, had participated in the Freedom Rides and almost had a nervous breakdown during the awful, violent summer of 1964 in Mississippi. In June 1966, he issued a call for "Black Power!" Carmichael never clearly explained what that slogan meant. He talked about economic and political power and in some ways echoed the philosophy of Malcolm X, the former minister of the Nation of Islam (the Black Muslims) who had been assassinated in 1965. While with the Nation, Malcolm X had called all whites "devils" and preached black separatism. After leaving the Nation, he had talked about cooperating with nonracist whites. But the general public had never forgotten his antiwhite speeches. Many people, black and white, also took Stokely Carmichael's Black Power! slogan to be a catchword for black violence.

The nonviolent civil rights movement was over. Important federal laws were in place that ended legal segregation. They had been won at a terrible price in lives and souls. On April 4, 1968, the most famous spokesman for nonviolence, Martin Luther King, Jr., was assassinated in Memphis, Tennessee, where he had gone to support striking black sanitation workers.

Over the next decades, African Americans made great strides in some areas of American life. Large numbers of African Americans exercised their new right to vote and elected scores of local and state representatives. Others took advantage of greater integration in education and housing. A substantial black middle class arose, in both the North and the South.

The end of legal segregation had unexpected effects on black America. Many historically black institutions suffered after blacks had the opportunity to participate in areas of white life from which they had previously been excluded. Some members of the new black middle class chose to attend white colleges, get jobs in white companies, move to white neighborhoods. As a result, black neighborhoods lost important role models.

Large numbers of blacks remain poor, and separate, unable to take advantage of the opportunities that had opened up for others. To many of them and their heirs, the Freedom Rides have meant little. But to others, rich and poor, black and white, the Freedom Rides remain a lasting symbol of the civil rights movement.

WHAT HAPPENED TO THE FREEDOM RIDERS?

In 1991, Tougaloo College in Mississippi hosted an event to mark the thirty-year anniversary of the original Freedom Ride. The reunion of former Freedom Riders was attended by Janie Forsyth Miller, in whose yard the Freedom Riders bus had burned in Anniston, Alabama. Twelve years old at the time, she had risked the displeasure of her white neighbors by taking water to the dazed and injured riders. She had left Anniston as soon as she graduated from high school. In fact, only her mother remained in Anniston.

Six of the original thirteen Freedom Riders were in attendance—John Lewis, Ed Blankenheim, Ike Reynolds, Henry Thomas, Jimmy McDonald, and the Reverend B. Elton Cox.

John Lewis, who in 1961 was a seminary student, became a major force in SNCC and participated in all the major civil rights campaigns that followed the Freedom Rides. Respect for his role as a tireless foot soldier in the civil rights movement helped him win election as a city councilman in Atlanta and, in 1989, as a member of the U.S. House of Representatives from his Atlanta district.

Altogether, Lewis was jailed forty times and beaten so often that in later years he suffered from a speech impediment.

"Forty times," he has said of the number of times he was

jailed. "Not for stealing, not for beating anybody up, not for using drugs."[1] Lewis is a man without bitterness. He does not complete the thought. But his listeners do: Not for committing crimes but for demonstrating for basic civil rights.

At the anniversary session in Tougaloo, some veterans of the Freedom Rides, among them Ed Blankenheim, were bitter as they remembered how whites had crowded around to watch the bus burn in Anniston: "Good old boys in pickup trucks with their wives and children, a treat for the children. If I sound bitter, perhaps I am."

For Henry Thomas, the experience had served as a source of strength. "When I left Anniston, I was mad as hell. I was determined to show them, walk down these streets as a proud, successful man." As he walked the streets of Anniston in 1991, he said, "You want to just tell people you're back."

Life had not always been easy for him in the intervening years. Drafted and sent to Vietnam early in the war (which the United States entered in the early 1960s), he went grudgingly. "I remember thinking, 'In Lowndes County, Alabama, I couldn't register to vote, but there I was on my way to fight for the rights of the Vietnamese.'"

Wounded in Vietnam, he returned to the United States and spent four months in a hospital ward. There, he listened to the white patients talk about their futures, realizing that he had many fewer options than they did. When one of them offered him a job, he determined that he would be his own boss. By 1991, he owned three McDonald's restaurants in Atlanta.

Back in 1961, Jimmy McDonald was a member of CORE and a folksinger of some renown. But the Freedom Rides experience caused him to rethink his plans for the future, making him determined to devote his life to the cause of human rights.

He went to work full-time as an organizer for CORE then, in the late 1960s, for SNCC. He later went into televis hosted two programs, *Black Journal* and *Black Perspective* (*News.* He also did a stint as executive director of the Human Commission in Yonkers, New York. In 1991, he was workin manager for the pianist Cecil Taylor.

Some who had been involved in the Freedom Rides attend the reunion in Mississippi. They did, however, appear event hosted at the Ripley Street First Baptist Church in Mont the former church of Ralph David Abernathy, where Freedon escaping from white mobs at the Montgomery bus station ha refuge thirty years before. Among them was John Seigentha in 1961 was an aide to Attorney General Robert Kennedy. H flown to Montgomery to assess the situation and on May 20 had been knocked unconscious when he tried to rescue a yo female Freedom Rider. Following the assassination of Presi John F. Kennedy, Seigenthaler had returned to the Nashville *Tennessean*, the newspaper where he had worked before goi Washington. He marked his forty-second year at the paper, he was chairman, publisher, and chief executive officer, in 1

Asked to ascend to the pulpit of the church and spea Seigenthaler protested that it was not appropriate for him to ored in the same way as those who had been in Montgomer different reasons. He was there, he explained, as a duty. But who had invited him believed he had made a contribution, t unlike many white southerners, he had possessed the human help someone he saw was in trouble.

It is safe to say that not one of the Freedom Riders same after the experience as he or she had been before. Eve who were not beaten were profoundly changed by the sheer

of putting their lives on the line, of riding into an unknown fate. Few escaped the rigors of prison or the utter hatred of the whites in Alabama and Mississippi.

For most, the wounds were inside—more psychic than physical. Selyn McCollum, who had been a student at Nashville's Peabody College in 1961 and who had been part of the first contingent of reinforcements from Nashville, found the experience somewhat traumatic. "It's a kind of personal confrontation," she explained. "How effective was my life?"

Bernard Lafayette, who was a twenty-year-old seminary student in Nashville when he joined the Freedom Rides, organized for SNCC in the 1960s. He then went to work for the SCLC, and Martin Luther King, Jr., appointed him national program director. Later, he served as national coordinator for King's Poor People's Campaign. After King's death, Lafayette helped organize the National Peace Institute in Washington, D.C., and the Martin Luther King Institute in New York. In 1991 he was vice president for academic affairs at American Baptist College in Nashville. He claimed that the Freedom Rides taught him a valuable lesson: "that by applying energy and thought, we could effect social change."

Some Freedom Riders suffered lasting physical damage.

Four months after the beatings he received at Anniston and Birmingham, Walter Bergman, the sixty-year-old Wayne State University professor, went into cardiac arrest, and he was confined to a wheelchair for the rest of his life. In 1975, a Senate committee obtained FBI documents through the Freedom of Information Act that revealed that an FBI informant in the Ku Klux Klan had told the agency of a plan to assault the Freedom Riders. Bergman and his wife, Frances, who had by this time retired to Grand Rapids, Michigan, sued the FBI for $2 million. Neurologists who testified

on their behalf said that Bergman's confinement to a wheelchair was a direct result of the beatings. In 1983 a federal judge agreed that the FBI should have stopped the violence. But he said that the medical evidence was not conclusive. He awarded Bergman $35,000 in damages. He awarded $15,000 to the estate of Frances Bergman, who had died in 1979. In 1989, the Michigan chapter of the American Civil Liberties Union published a book entitled *The First Freedom Ride: The Walter Bergman Story*. Bergman was

1983, Kalamazoo, Michigan. Walter Bergman (left) with friend Isaac Reynolds during Bergman's lawsuit against the FBI.

eighty-nine at the time and still convinced that he had done the right thing, no matter what it had cost him. "I feel that my participation and that of my fellow Freedom Riders has changed the South," he said. "I think it was the most useful thing I've done. . . . And that's what keeps me content to roll around in my wheelchair and feel no regrets."[2]

James Peck, who was beaten along with Bergman in Anniston and Birmingham, and then beaten again in Montgomery, also sued the FBI, in 1976. In 1983, a federal judge in New York awarded him $25,000. After the Freedom Rides, he had continued his work in the civil rights and labor movements. Author of a book on pacifism, *We Who Would Not Kill*, which was published in the 1950s, he also wrote an account of his Freedom Ride experience, entitled *Freedom Ride*, which appeared in the middle 1960s. In the 1970s his book *Upper Dog Versus Underdog* was published.

Peck suffered a stroke in 1983 and was unable to be physically active in the various causes to which he had devoted his life. But he still stuffed envelopes for Amnesty International, a worldwide human rights organization. Not long after his stroke, he said, "My life has been nonviolent direct action to try to make this a better world. It is my philosophy that the struggle has to be a nonending one, because I am not one of those idealists who envision a utopia."[3] James Peck died in 1993 at the age of seventy-eight.

Diane Nash has expressed similar feelings. Not long after the Freedom Rides, she married fellow SNCC member the Reverend James Bevel. After SNCC renounced nonviolence, the two joined the SCLC, where both held leadership positions and continued their nonviolent activism. In that capacity, they worked closely with Dr. Martin Luther King, Jr. They loved and respected King, but Diane Nash Bevel believes that the image of King has come to overshadow the entire civil rights movement. She knows from personal experience that the movement was the work of thousands of less heralded people. As she told David J. Garrow, author of the 1986 book *Bearing the Cross: Martin Luther King, Jr., and the Southern Christian Leadership Conference,* "If people think that it was Martin Luther King's movement, then today they—young people—are more likely to say, 'Gosh, I wish we had a Martin Luther King here today to lead us.' . . . If people knew how that movement started, then the question they would ask themselves is, 'What can I do?' "[4]

James Farmer, whose Congress of Racial Equality initiated the Freedom Rides, continued to serve as CORE's national director until 1966 and was regarded as one of the "Big Six" of the civil rights movement. (The others were Martin Luther King, Jr., of the SCLC, Roy Wilkins of the NAACP, Whitney M. Young, Jr., of the National Urban League, John Lewis of SNCC, and A. Philip Randolph, founder of the Brotherhood of Sleeping Car Porters.) Farmer left CORE expecting to head a major adult-literacy drive, but federal funding for the drive was blocked by President Lyndon Johnson at the last moment. In 1968, he ran for Congress from the new Twelfth Congressional District in Brooklyn against Shirley Chisholm, who won the election to become the first black woman to serve in the U.S. House of Representatives. President Richard M. Nixon, the Republican winner of the 1968 presidential election, appointed Farmer an assistant secretary in the Department of Health, Education, and Welfare. Feeling increasingly uncomfortable in an administration that had very few black officeholders, Farmer resigned after two years.

From 1975 to 1981, Farmer served as executive director of the Coalition of American Public Employees. Suffering from a rare eye ailment—retinal vascular occlusion—that destroyed the sight in one eye in 1979, Farmer moved to Virginia, where he taught at Virginia State University part-time and wrote *Lay Bare the Heart: An Autobiography of the Civil Rights Movement*. Published in 1985, it was hailed by critics as one of the most honest and self-critical books ever written by a civil rights movement leader. In addition to regretting his fears for his own personal safety during the Freedom Rides, Farmer admitted, "The greatest tactical oversight of my life was that I did not at that time move for a merger between CORE and SNCC." That step "would have unified and given those activists a stronger foundation against efforts to undercut them."

CHAPTER ELEVEN

THE LEGACY OF THE FREEDOM RIDES

The Freedom Rides were a brief moment in the civil rights movement, but they captured the attention of the nation in a way that few
other campaigns in the struggle had. They especially inspired southern blacks. For several years afterward, anytime a southern black
encountered a civil rights worker, he or she was likely to ask, "Are
you one of them Freedom Riders?" It didn't matter if the worker
was registering voters or leading a sit-in demonstration. The term
Freedom Rider came to mean civil rights worker, especially to
southern blacks.

Mary King was a white SNCC worker who worked in a
voter-registration drive in Tougaloo during Mississippi Freedom
Summer, 1964. "The community surrounding Tougaloo College
called us Freedom Riders," she wrote in her 1987 book *Freedom
Song*. "Local black communities had been stunned by the daring of
the Freedom Rides of 1961 into the mob-packed segregated bus sta-
tions of Anniston, Birmingham, Montgomery, and finally into
Jackson. For years afterward, the local people in southern hamlets
called any and all civil rights workers by the stock name Freedom
Riders. Throughout the Alabama and Mississippi Black Belt, the
Rides had been such a shocking challenge to the old order that even

though Casey [her co-worker, Sandra Cason] and I never rode a bus and always drove to the Jackson office in a donated car, we were 'Freedom Riders' to the people of Tougaloo."[1]

That was the most important legacy of the Freedom Rides. Although they were crucial as a "shocking challenge to the old order," as absolute proof that thousands of people were willing to put their lives on the line and face pain and death for what they believed in, and as the harbingers of a new era of confrontation in the fight for civil rights, they were decisive in making the previously scattered attacks on segregation a true *movement*. As Taylor Branch writes in *Parting the Waters*, out of those Mississippi jails arose a civil rights "'movement' in both senses of the word—a moving spiritual experience and a steady expansion of scope. The theater was spreading through the entire South. One isolated battle had given way to many scattered ones, and now in the Mississippi jails they were moving from similar experiences to a common experience. Students began to think of the movement as a vocation in itself."[2]

Students, black and white, flocked to the South to launch voter-registration drives, to start informal adult-education schools, to harness the potential political power of the millions of black southerners. The emotional wave would not ebb until this power—both the moral power of the rightness of the campaign and the political power of the long-silent black voices—forced the U.S. government to pass laws guaranteeing equal rights for all.

E N D N O T E S

Chapter Two: The 1947 Journey of Reconciliation
1. James Farmer, *Lay Bare the Heart: An Autobiography of the Civil Rights Movement.* New York: Arbor House, 1985, p. 109.
2. Bayard Rustin, *Down the Line: The Collected Writings of Bayard Rustin.* Chicago: Quadrangle Books, 1971, p. 13.
   (All further quotations from Rustin's diary are from the same source.)
3. Bayard Rustin Interviews, Columbia University Oral History Project, Columbia University, New York, transcription p. 300.
4. Ibid., p. 292.

Chapter Four: The Montgomery Bus Boycott of 1955
1. Rosa Parks, *Rosa Parks: My Story, with Jim Haskins.* New York: Dial Books, 1992, pp. 108–9.
2. Ibid., p. 113.
3. Ibid., p. 116.
4. Ibid., p. 133.

Chapter Five: The Civil Rights Movement Begins
1. *Washington Post,* 6 March 1990, p. A3.

Chapter Six: The Freedom Rides Begin
1. Juan Williams, ed., *Eyes on the Prize: America's Civil Rights Years, 1954–1965.* New York: Viking Penguin, 1987, p. 147.
2. Taylor Branch, *Parting the Waters: America in the King Years, 1954–63.* New York: Simon & Schuster, 1988, p. 417.
3. Ibid., p. 419.

Chapter Seven: The Freedom Rides Continue
1. Farmer, p. 2.
2. Branch, p. 472.
3. Farmer, p. 3.
4. Ibid., p. 5.

Chapter Eight: The Freedom Riders in Jail
1. Farmer, p. 14.
2. Branch, p. 477.
3. *Los Angeles Times*, 11 February 1989, p. 1. (All further Filner quotations are from this source.)

Chapter Ten: What Happened to the Freedom Riders?
1. *Washington Post*, 6 March 1990.
2. Gannett News Service, 3 May 1991.
3. *New York Times*, 13 July 1993.
4. David J. Garrow, *Bearing the Cross: Martin Luther King, Jr., and the Southern Christian Leadership Conference.* New York: Morrow, 1986, p. 625.

Chapter Eleven: The Legacy of the Freedom Rides
1. Mary King, *Freedom Song: A Personal Story of the 1960s Civil Rights Movement.* New York: Morrow, 1987, p. 402.
2. Branch, p. 485.

B I B L I O G R A P H Y

BOOKS

Branch, Taylor. *Parting the Waters: America in the King Years 1954–63.* New York: Simon & Schuster, 1988.

Farmer, James. *Lay Bare the Heart: An Autobiography of the Civil Rights Movement.* New York: Arbor House, 1985.

Garrow, David J. *Bearing the Cross: Martin Luther King, Jr., and the Southern Christian Leadership Conference.* New York: Morrow, 1986.

Haskins, James. *The March on Washington.* New York: HarperCollins, 1993.

———. *Thurgood Marshall: A Life for Justice.* New York: Holt, 1992.

King, Mary. *Freedom Song: A Personal Story of the 1960s Civil Rights Movement.* New York: Morrow, 1987.

McKissack, Patricia, and Fredrick McKissack. *The Civil Rights Movement in America from 1865 to the Present.* Chicago: Children's Press, 1987.

Parks, Rosa, with Jim Haskins. *Rosa Parks: My Story.* New York: Dial Books, 1992.

Rustin, Bayard. *Down the Line: The Collected Writings of Bayard Rustin.* Chicago: Quadrangle Books, 1971.

Tushnet, Mark V. *The NAACP's Legal Strategy Against Segregated Education, 1925–1950.* Chapel Hill: University of North Carolina Press, 1987.

Williams, Juan, ed. *Eyes on the Prize: America's Civil Rights Years, 1954–1965.* New York: Viking Penguin, 1987.

PERIODICALS

Bernstein, Leonard, "Memory of Prison Cell Shapes Filner's Views of Rights Film," *Los Angeles Times Calendar,* 11 February 1989, p. 5.

Daniel, Leon, "Lawmaker Paid His Dues in Blood," United Press International, 4 June 1991.

Douglas, William, "Freedom Riders Are Welcomed Home," *Newsday,* 25 June 1989, p. 19.

"Freedom Riders," United Press International, 24 July 1981.

Garrow, David J., review of *Lay Bare the Heart: An Autobiography of the Civil Rights Movement* by James Farmer, *The Nation,* 4 May 1985, p. 535.

Hewitt, John A. "The Search for Elizabeth Jennings, Heroine of a Sunday Afternoon in New York City," *New York History* (October 1990): 387–415.

"Judge Orders Government to Release Documents," United Press International, 4 March 1983.

Lubasch, Arnold H., "Ex-Freedom Rider Sues U.S." *New York Times,* 23 January 1983.

Maddux, Barbara, and Loudon Wainwright, "Out of Despair," *Time,* Spring 1988 Special Issue, p. 8.

May, Lee, "Past Meets Future in Mississippi," *Los Angeles Times,* 22 June 1989, p. 1.

Mayfield, Mark, "Black, White Freedom Riders: After 30 Years, Battles Remain," Gannett News Service, 3 May 1991.

Milloy, Marilyn, "In Mississippi, A Freedom Ride of Remembrance," *Newsday,* 21 June 1989, p. 4.

Nossiter, Adam, "Freedom Riders Look Back at '61," *Atlanta Journal and Constitution,* 19 July 1991, p. 10.

_____, "Freedom Riders Remain a Breed Apart," *Atlanta Journal and Constitution,* 21 July 1991, p. 3.

_____, "On the Highway to Freedom," *Atlanta Journal and Constitution,* 19 July 1991, p. 3.

Parker, Laura, "John Lewis: Scarred Survivor Brings Home Lessons of '60s," *Washington Post,* 6 March 1990, p. A3.

Reynolds, Rachel, "The Life of a Freedom Rider," Gannett News Service, 23 February 1990.

Rice, Yanick, "Civil Rights Reunion," *New York Times,* 10 April 1988, 12CN, p. 14.

Smith, Shirley L., "A 'Freedom' Ride to the Mountaintop," *Atlanta Journal and Constitution,* 10 January 1993, p. 6.

Stuart, Reginald, "Freedom Riders Find Pride and Pain on '61 Route," *New York Times,* 10 May 1981, p. 1.

Swirka, Gregory, "Freedom," Gannett News Service, 15 May 1989.

Wickham, DeWayne, "Civil Rights Veteran Takes Turn at Pulpit," Gannett News Service, 19 July 1991.

Williams, Juan, "Have We Forgotten the Dream?" *Washington Post*, 22 February 1987, p. C1.

Wilmer, Val, "Early Days of Rage." *The Independent,* 22 November 1992, p. 9.

OTHER SOURCES

James Peck obituary, *New York Times,* 13 July 1993.

Bayard Rustin Interviews. Columbia University Oral History Project, Columbia University, New York.